HOW TO MAKE INSURANCE COMPANIES PAY YOUR CLAIMS

HOW TO MAKE INSURANCE COMPANIES PAY YOUR CLAIMS

&

What to Do If They Don't

WILLIAM M. SHERNOFF, *Attorney*

FOREWORD BY RALPH NADER

HASTINGS HOUSE ☐ *MAMARONECK, NEW YORK*

ISBN 0-8038-9325-6

Cover design by Rob Pawlak

Printed in the United States by Hastings House, Book Publishers, 141 Halstead Avenue, Mamaroneck, NY 10543

Distributed by Publishers Group West, Emeryville, California

Contents

Foreword

by Ralph Nader

Did you ever try to read those obscure paragraphs in your insurance policy? Did you understand them? Did you ever wonder why they weren't written in clear, simple language? The chances are that you accepted the obscurity and difficult language as just the way these matters have always been. You bought your policy based on the good faith of your insurance company.

Suppose the obscure language is put there to confuse you?

And, when you have a legitimate claim, what makes you believe your insurance company will deal with you in good faith?

The average consumer spends 12 cents out of every income dollar on insurance; therefore, one would expect some kind of government regulation over this multibillion-dollar industry. Indeed, every state has an insurance department, whose mandate is to regulate and supervise the insurance industry. But, in most instances, state regulation is a farce. Even if the agencies were anxious to protect you in the first place, state agencies have few actuaries or professional staff members to check insurance-company abuse.

In only two or three states at any given time are there insurance commissioners with the desire to curb abuse. Commissioners, selected because of their knowledge of the industry, often have close ties to the industry. The annual meetings of the National Association of Insurance Commissioners (NAIC) are replete with hotel hospitality suites and evenings of entertainment hosted by insurance groups or companies— the very companies the commissioners are supposed to regulate. And this is where hordes of insurance executives, lobbyists, and public-relations specialists lavish attention on the state commissioners and their staffs.

Concerned about this state of affairs, late in 1983 consumer groups appealed to NAIC to appoint a consumer advisory committee to balance the avalanche of one-sided information pouring out of the insurance companies.

NAIC turned it down.

If the insurance departments of the various states do not wish to concern themselves with the rights of the consumers—what, if anything, is their function? That is the multibillion-dollar question. The answer is self-evident.

During World War II, the United States Supreme Court ruled that insurance was an interstate business and therefore within federal regulatory purview. But the insurance industry is so powerful that it flexed its lobbying muscles and secured legislation through Congress in 1945 (the McCarran-Ferguson Act) taking the federal government out of insurance regulation.

Too many insurance companies are crass, profit-oriented, and specialize in "bad faith" relationships with the consumer. They engage in all-out battles with the policyholder in two areas:

(a) behind the scenes as lobbyists; and

(b) when policyholders try to collect on legitimate claims.

For the past thirteen years, members of Congress have tried to enact legislation to compel greater insurance disclosure to consumers. Disclosure would enable consumers to comparison-shop and obtain the best buy—much as in buying a car. But the industry is so powerful that it has successfully bottled up this effort. It even went so far as to get Congress *to curtail the right of the Federal Trade Commission to study the industry.* Fortunately, now the General Accounting Office (the investigative arm of Congress) is assessing the inadequacies of state regulation.

Not only is it difficult for the consumer to comparison-shop policies of different companies, but the industry has blocked other sources of competition which could reduce the rate of your insurance. In all 50 states, insurance agents are prohibited from discounting their premiums to get your business. And in 37 states, you and your neighbors are prohibited from getting together as a group and buying—at a lower price—a group homeowners' insurance policy.

But a major problem with insurance companies is the legitimate claim. Whether it is a fire in your home, a work-related disability, or an accident covered by your insurance policy, the question is: Will you collect?

Despite what is written in your policy, the judge of whether you'll be paid is the claims adjuster—not the insurance agent or insurance sales department, who may have been taking your money five, ten, or even twenty years. The claims adjuster has the power to pay, settle, or not pay at all.

So what happens when your honest claim is turned down?

When small claims are rejected by the adjuster, most people give up in disgust. *This is exactly what the insurance companies want you to do.* Think about the millions of honest claims that are never challenged, and you can understand the surge of wealth generated by most major insurance companies. An angry consumer may seek redress from the state insurance commissioner, but, as explained earlier, this is rarely effective.

Or you can take the insurance company to court.

The person who has rattled more nonpaying insurance companies than anyone else in the country is attorney William Shernoff. His specialty is going after insurance companies who demonstrate "bad faith" in dealing with policyholders. He has won many cases for compensatory and punitive damages for clients who have paid their premium faithfully—only to find that they had to fight their insurance companies to collect on their injuries. In one case, when Shernoff was able to demonstrate that a major insurance company acted in "bad faith" when it turned down a simple claim, the jury awarded the policyholder $8 million in punitive damages.

While many claims are settled for smaller amounts of money, newspaper and TV coverage of blatant cases have alerted consumers of their rights when they buy insurance coverage.

In this book, Shernoff brings to your attention the unfair policies practiced by these insurance companies. In a series of dramatic case histories, you follow Shernoff as he argues each case before a judge and jury—stripping away the obscure paragraphs and confusing language that insurance companies believe give them license to turn down honest claims.

Take the case of Mike Egan, an Irish immigrant in his early fifties who hurt his back when he fell off a roof. Charging that he was malingering, Mutual of Omaha decided it would make no further payments after three months. Or take the case of Joe Ingram, who injured his back on the job. He believed he was covered under a credit disability policy with Commercial Bankers Life Insurance Company. The company decided otherwise.

Ray Pistorius was a long- and short-haul trucker who was injured in an accident just twelve days after he increased his disability policy with Prudential Insurance Company. After months of paying on his claim, the nation's largest insurer suddenly decided to discontinue paying him his monthly benefits.

Ultimately these plaintiffs won their cases. But many policyholders have paid premiums only to discover that they have been turned down on their claims. It is no wonder that in some states, notably California, the courts have been mindful of the people with legitimate claims who have been refused payment. This is the reason for the punitive-damage awards: the high cash awards that punish the insurance companies for refusing to honor their policies. It is a message by the courts that disreputable claims practices must be stopped.

Shernoff feels strongly about the matter. He points out, correctly, that a policyholder who defrauds an insurance company ends up in prison, but an insurance company official who defrauds a consumer is not even subject to prosecution.

In the absence of organized bargaining power by policyholders, taking companies to court and obtaining punitive-damage awards help fill the void. However, more effective action could be taken by legislative bodies if they would only read the depositions of company officials testifying in court; they verify in their own words how they hoodwink the policyholder.

By law, insurance companies are "fiduciaries," which means they are founded on public trust. They employ actuaries who calculate and anticipate the income versus claims against the company. This results in a reasonable profit for the insurance companies. However, by a change in outlook, insurance companies decided that they are profit centers. This attitude enabled them to deny or cut down on paying legitimate claims or harass policyholders in order to achieve greater profits. This is a betrayal of trust.

Case by case, Shernoff and other attorneys who battle the "bad faith" of the insurance industry are building the legal shield to protect you from mistreatment.

This book is an important milestone in the fight for consumer rights. It was written so that you may know and
understand these rights when you buy an insurance policy.
Now, in the pages of this absorbing book, read how interesting the struggle for these rights can be.

RALPH NADER
Washington, D.C.

Editorial Note

Because of the enormous amounts of court testimony and records required to prepare this book, contractions and excerpts have been made for editorial purposes and reasons of clarity. But in no way has the sense or meaning of any testimony been intentionally changed.

Some material from William Shernoff's earlier book, *Payment Refused*, was used in the writing of this book.

Acknowledgments

I wish to thank my son, David Shernoff, presently at Harvard Graduate School, for an excellent job in doing the research on and writing the first three chapters of this book. It was certainly nice for me to have such superb help from Dave, who took a keen interest in digging up vital information necessary to explain difficult insurance concepts and reducing them to clear, plain English.

I also want to extend my hearty thanks to Robert D. San Souci, who did a tremendous job of editing. Many thanks go to Hy Steirman of Hastings House and Julie Bennett of Publishers Group West for helping me get this book launched. My agent, Peter Miller, is owed thanks for continually being supportive.

I would be remiss if I did not acknowledge with gratitude my clients, who allowed me to pursue their causes; my office staff, especially my efficient secretaries, Nancy Burnett and Diane Messrah; and the many consumer rights lawyers across the country who have helped me throughout my career.

Lastly, I should not forget my heroes who have been inspirational—Ralph Nader, the undisputed world heavyweight champion of consumer causes, and Robert Hunter, president of the National Insurance Consumer Organization. Both have inspired me to keep working, in the arena of the courthouse, for the cause of consumerism in the area of insurance.

HOW TO MAKE INSURANCE COMPANIES PAY YOUR CLAIMS

CHAPTER 1

What You Should Know Before Making Your Claim

I

INTRODUCTION—DON'T SLEEP ON YOUR RIGHTS

It's your worst nightmare come true.

Little Johnny was playing with matches again. Thank God Johnny is all right, but unfortunately you cannot say the same thing about your home, which would be better described as a giant heap of ashes. After temporary spasms of panic and grief, you try to get hold of yourself. "It's okay. It's okay," you console yourself. "Insurance will take care of it, right?"

"Right?" you ask your friendly insurance agent.

"Yes, of course," he says. "Just calm down and let me ask you a few questions. Now then, what was your policy number?"

"Well, my policy was destroyed in the fire." This, of course, is just as well, since you never read your policy and have long since forgotten where you kept it.

"Yes, I see," he says. "Well, then, do you have any

receipts for your household possessions? You know—TV, microwave, that sort of thing?"

"No, sir. I'm afraid that's all gone, too." Of course, you are referring to the total sum of all your saved receipts—those from your last three grocery sprees which had not yet been thrown out with the other household clutter. You start to get nervous. You are sweating. You can't take it anymore.

You grab the friendly insurance agent by his shoulders and shake him. "Listen, please, just tell me what I'm covered for," you demand.

Your friendly agent manages to loosen himself from your grip and straighten his attire, then sips his coffee to regain a sense of dignity. He smiles and begins his rehearsed monologue: "Don't worry. Fill out these forms stating the description and value of every item that was in your house. Just send it in, and we will figure it all out. You shouldn't have to worry over your insurance coverage at a stressful time like this. That's for us to decide. Don't worry, we pay for most things. There aren't too many exclusions. Just leave everything to us. You can trust us."

If you are like most people, you follow this friendly bit of advice all too readily. You take a back seat and watch your insurance company as it drives you on a dark and twisting road toward your settlement. While you may not feel completely comfortable with such a passive position, you have put yourself here by skimming a policy prior to purchase—and not taking care to review and update your property lists. You have not even kept a record that will survive a fire. But you won't take any flack from your insurance company for your lackadaisical attitude: insurance companies are counting on your back-seat attitude. They would not have it any other way. A policyholder who lets his or her insurance company manage the settlement process is likely to accept whatever is offered without challenge.

Returning to our example of the house destroyed by fire:

the owners may well find themselves plunging deep into a nightmare of unexpected exclusions, reduced compensation for lost household goods, and a total redress that is far below what is necessary to rebuild or purchase a similar structure in the same area. Unfamiliar with what a policy guaranteed, and all too willing to accept an insurance company's say-so, a policyholder may find himself or herself stranded in untenable financial and living circumstances.

This does not have to be the case. This book can help put consumers like you into the driver's seat, where you belong. It can keep you from facing an insurance nightmare such as the one just described.

At the outset, a potential or actual policyholder must realize some very basic facts. For one thing, your insurance claim is much more important to you than it is to your insurance company. If you have ever been a victim of a major theft, fire, accident, or injury, you know how much you depend on prompt and reasonable compensation. You have good reason to be the most concerned party. You cannot rely on the graciousness and benevolence of your insurance company to go out of its way for your maximum protection. This is not to say that insurance companies never handle claims fairly and properly if left to their own devices. Most insurance companies are very concerned with customer satisfaction, and therefore they are likely to handle a claim in a manner that they deem reasonable and fair. However, what most people do not realize is that:

Your Interpretation of What Is Fair May Be Different from Your Insurance Company's Interpretation.

It is important to remember that insurance is a business, and a very big business at that. This means that the profit motive is going to be the driving force behind how insurance companies conduct their business. For insurance companies, one of the best ways to increase profits is to decrease payment of claims, though your insurance company is probably not out to blatantly cheat you of what you deserve,

Most Companies Will Be Reluctant to Pay What They Do Not Have to Pay.

They feel that it simply makes good business sense to pay no more than the lowest legal amount—or not to pay at all, if a claim can be denied on "reasonable" grounds. Therefore, it is up to you to make them pay. If you are not going to stick up for your rights, do you think they will?

Sleeping on your rights is unhealthy for you, your family, and society. The purpose of this book is to make you aware of certain valuable rights and to show you how average citizens have used these rights effectively. As one of the persons portrayed in this book said from her deathbed, "We are victims because we allow ourselves to become victims." She had valiantly contested to the end her own insurer's denial of certain claims she asserted were due her. Though the final decision—in her favor—came after her death, her words should be a warning to anyone who is tempted, through ignorance or inertia, to shrug off a seemingly unfair settlement.

Such a failure to learn—and exercise—one's insurance rights has far-reaching implications. Exercising your rights is extremely significant to you and your family because, without the knowledge and ability to fight back, you increase the risk of becoming a victim of insurance abuse. Doing nothing pretty much guarantees that you will come out a sure loser if it becomes necessary to file a claim. On the other hand, being able to handle yourself effectively will probably get you what is rightly due to you and, in some cases of insurance abuse, even more in punitive damages, imposed as a form of punishment on the offending company.

More importantly, we are in an era of heavy emphasis on a free marketplace unregulated by government controls. This is true particularly of the insurance industry. The only way for a free marketplace to stay healthy indefinitely is to have a mechanism for catching and punishing those who abuse this privilege. This means that you, the consumer—when you become a victim—have a duty to society to exercise your rights. By so doing, you keep our free marketplace honest and healthy.

One of the best ways to keep from becoming a victim is to be prepared for the worst. The remainder of this chapter is designed to help you improve your insurance posture so that you do not find yourself in a helpless state of affairs when you file an insurance claim.

II
BUYING YOUR INSURANCE POLICY

It may seem like stating the obvious to say that it is a good idea to do some comparative shopping for insurance policies. But the importance of this cannot be overstressed. As different policies vary in price and coverage, it may take a little bit of time before you find a policy that suits your particular needs.

One of the best ways to compare policies is simply to call various insurance agents and inquire about a particular policy. You may want to keep a running list of the different premiums and benefits that are offered by several major insurance companies. It may also be helpful to talk it over with friends or family before making a purchase. You might want to find out what kinds of policies they have, and how satisfied they have been with them.

If you want to be more rigorous in your comparison, there have been several articles featured in *Consumer Reports* and other consumer magazines which compare the policies of insurance companies for many lines of insurance. Another very good resource for such "comparison shopping" is your State Department of Insurance. Many State Departments are beginning to gather an impressive amount of information comparing insurance companies with regard to prices as well as the number of complaints filed against them. (For more information on State Departments of Insurance, see Chapter 3.)

One golden piece of advice when buying an insurance policy:

Always Buy Your Insurance Policies From Reputable Insurance Companies.

Do not make the mistake of buying insurance policies from any type of "offbeat" or "unestablished" insurance company, for they have been known to go bankrupt. The A. M. Best Company publishes several reports and rating guides which contain financial and other important information bearing on the reliability of all insurance companies doing business in the United States. Their address is: A. M. Best Company, Oldwick, New Jersey 08858, (201) 439-2200.

The two basic Best guides are *Best's Key Rating Guide* and *Best's Trend Report*. These list insurance companies alphabetically and explain the Best ratings system (which works much like a school grading system, with A+ being the best rating). You may well get all the information you need from these two books.

Two more complicated guides are *Best's Insurance Re-*

ports: Property—Casualty and *Best's Insurance Reports: Life—Health,* which put each insurance company together with its affiliated companies; entries are listed under the name of the insurance group. Many insurance companies conduct business using a variety of legal entities, affiliated companies, and so forth. These books will help you see the characteristics of the organization behind your insurance company. The *Insurance Reports* gives tables listing the states in which the various insurers are licensed and contains other useful information.

You want to entrust your money to a fairly well known and established insurance company for the same reason you would do this with a bank—security. This is, after all, the purpose of insurance.

There are a couple of tips it may be wise to remember when dealing with insurance agents. First of all, know the qualifications of anyone selling you an insurance policy. Many states require that agents carry licenses displaying their name and the company they represent. If an agent cannot show you proof of licensure upon request, buy your policy from someone who can.

If your agent makes any promises about future benefits, coverage, or prices when selling you an insurance policy, ask where these promises exist in the text of the policy itself. If your agent cannot point out where these guarantees exist within the policy, ask that he or she put such promises *in writing.* All too often consumers think they are covered for something when they're not because, they say, "My agent told me so." This is not good enough. To avoid unpleasant surprises at a later date, it is best to make sure everything is spelled out from the first.

This next tip is a rule of thumb to apply in all phases of your dealings with insurance companies:

Keep Copies of Everything: Everything You Sign, Everything Your Agent Signs, All Payments, All Receipts, and All Correspondence.

The importance of keeping good documentation cannot be stressed enough. This becomes particularly important in the latter stages of filing a claim, as will be discussed in later chapters. For now, make sure to keep copies of your policy and all signed materials in a safe place. The importance of keeping good records is the main reason you should pay for your insurance by check and make the check payable to the company, as cases have arisen where an agent or agency has neglected to forward the funds to the company. Finally, always get receipts signed and dated by your agent as proof of payment.

One of the current abuses in the insurance industry targets senior citizens on Medicare who frequently buy "Medigap" policies. Medigap policies are offered by health insurance companies to supplement Medicare benefits. That is, they cover "gaps" in Medicare programs. In 1986, an estimated four out of five senior citizens had policies to supplement their Medicare coverage. Abusive practices in selling Medigap insurance have included false advertising or solicitations designed to resemble authentic correspondence from Medicare or the federal government; exaggerating benefits and omitting important exclusions in promotional literature and TV ads; and selling multiple, unnecessary, or overlapping policies. Senior citizens who unwittingly trust unscrupulous insurance agents or who feel pressured from an agent to buy needless policies often fall victims. If you have questions about Medigap abuse, contact your State Department of Insurance. (See Chapter 3.)

III
UNDERSTANDING YOUR POLICY

Insurance policies can be boring, tedious, and confusing to review, but the best way to help yourself is to:

Just Read It, and Pay Special Attention to the "Coverages," the "Exclusions," and the "Definitions of Terms"

Do not wait to read your insurance policy. Reading it is the only way to assure yourself that the contract between you and your insurance company is what you expected. Perhaps the main reason that people think they have more coverage than they actually have is that so many put their policy away after purchasing it and never bother to read it. *This is a very big mistake.* By the time you need to act on your policy, it will be too late to change it. Most companies will not alter your coverage after the fact.

Spend at least 20 minutes or so going over the policy to see what is and is not covered. Make sure to read the face sheet (declarations page) to verify that you have the coverage you expected. Then read any important *definitions* contained in the policy carefully.

If you are unsure about any of the definitions, or in any way confused about the terms of the coverage, call your agent to double-check and ask what the unclear definition means.

Next,

Read the "Exclusions" Very Carefully.

Most claim denials are based on clauses or phrases called "exclusions." These are little gems that usually appear on the last several pages of your policy and take away the coverage that appears on the first couple of pages. Because many people are unaware of these exclusions and the exclusions are difficult to understand, most courts have added this rule to aid the policyholder:

Exclusions in Any Insurance Policy Must Be Phrased in Plain, Clear, and Conspicuous Language. The Burden Is on the Insurance Company to Prove That the Exclusion Applies and That It Is Clear and Understandable.

Most people do not even bother to read an insurance policy carefully until it comes time to make a claim. One reason (aside from simple carelessness) is that, for many average consumers, it seems as though the comprehension level required to understand most policies is slightly higher than that needed to understand Einstein's theory of relativity. The policyholder starts out at a disadvantage. The insurance company deliberately writes a policy which is difficult to understand, and the company will probably interpret the language to its advantage. While this may be so, here is an important legal rule that your insurance company won't tell you that applies to all insurance jargon:

Courts Have Held That Where Insurance Policy Language Is Unclear, the Language Will Be Construed Against the Insurance Company.

This rule has been around for over a hundred years and means that where language is capable of two different meanings, *the policyholder's interpretation will prevail.* What this means is that, in a dispute, you do not take the insurance company's word for the meaning of certain language and phrases in the policy. Stick to your guns if you believe that your interpretation of the language is reasonable. Within the last ten years, some courts have gone even further by holding that:

The Reasonable Expectations of the Policyholder Will Govern the Meaning of the Policy Language.

This simply means that you get the coverage you expected, so long as your expectation was reasonable. This coverage may exist regardless of some fine print in the policy that may seem contrary.

As you can see, the courts have constructed rules to aid the policyholder. This is because most insurance policies are what the law calls "adhesion" contracts. These are contracts where there is no bargaining. The company offers you a policy on a take-it-or-leave-it basis, and you have no say-so as to what goes into the language of the contract. The traditional idea of a contract as being a "meeting of the minds," reflecting a give-and-take hammering-out of the terms of the contract between buyer and seller, gets tossed out the window. Do not forget that most insurance adjusters obviously have superior knowledge of insurance, and therefore it is extremely important that you have some understanding of the basic rules of insurance interpretation.

IV
THE ENDLESS LOOPHOLES (SOME HEALTH INSURANCE EXCLUSIONS)

As already indicated, exclusions are loopholes in your insurance policy that have the power to reduce your coverage. Let us take a look at the many colorful and creative ways insurance companies commonly use the language of the policy to avoid making payments, as well as tips you can use to combat these excuses. Remember, insurance companies will not pay if they do not have to pay.

When you file a claim, your insurance company will review the claim in light of a series of questions to determine whether or not the claim is "payable." Question number one: "Is the policy in force?" If the policy has expired or premium payments have been neglected, your company may conclude that your policy was out of force and immediately deny payment. For this reason, it is strongly recommended that you:

Do Not Be Late with Your Insurance Payments.

Most people are used to having a certain "grace period" when paying their bills. Landlords are unlikely to throw their tenants out on the streets for being a couple of days late with the rent. However, you cannot always rely on such a grace period when dealing with insurance companies. If you are five days late with your premium payment and you become injured two days after your payment (or even worse, before you got the chance to pay at all), your insurance company can use your tardiness to resist payment.

Question number two: "Are you eligible?" In other words, are you covered by the policy? This question is most often asked in group health insurance policies. This issue may be resolved as quickly as checking a list of eligibility. If your company wrongfully decides that you are ineligible, enlist the help of your employer or any third-party administrator handling the group policy.

Assuming your claim passes these first two tests, and that you are found to be an eligible claimant of a policy in force, your company will then look to determine whether or not the expense is covered by the policy. This is where exclusions come in.

Let us use health insurance as an example. Let's say that you wake up one morning with a terribly painful and mysterious eye infection, maybe something akin to a common case of "pinkeye." You go to your ophthalmologist for an eye examination, and he gives you a prescription for some medication. Within a couple of days, the medication has cleared up the problem. When you're feeling better, you submit your medical bill to your insurance company. Let's consider some common health insurance exclusions and some reasons for denial of payment that you might encounter.

Routine Checkups versus Diagnosis

Your insurance company may decide that your eye appointment was a routine checkup, which is excluded in the policy. Many insurers won't pay for general medical checkups. If they see anything that looks like part of a routine checkup, such as screening tests or eye examinations, the company is likely to withhold payment. To avoid any possible confusion, you should be careful to show that the bill is in fact part of a medically necessary treatment or is otherwise related to a legitimate medical problem. The best way to do this is to:

Be Specific in Describing the Nature of Your Treatment on the Claims Form.

Merely writing "eye examination" is not good enough. Write down the diagnosis and the specific treatment prescribed for the medical condition.

Medical Necessity

Your insurance company may determine that your eye treatment was not medically necessary even if your doctor recommended the procedure. (See Chapter 7 for a good example of this problem.) Other examples: (1) Most policies will not pay for any procedures or surgery that are considered cosmetic, such as plastic surgery, but should pay if the procedure is reconstructive surgery in connection with other treatment, such as a mastectomy. (2) The company says the procedure was experimental and hence not covered. (3) The company claims some days you were hospitalized were unnecessary because you could have been released sooner.

Obviously, you should not be held financially responsible. However, these examples show that there is some confusion over what is medically necessary. In a recent case, one insurance company held that the surgical replacement of their insured's outer ear—lost through an accident—was only cosmetic. Again, you may have to go out of your way to show that the procedure was necessary for your health. If you and your insurer still disagree over the necessity of the procedure, get more opinions from other doctors. In the last analysis, it should be your doctor's opinion, not the insurance company's, of what is medically necessary that should be the deciding factor. After all, doctors practice medicine— insurance companies don't.

The Reasonable and Customary Clause

Many policies pay for 80 percent of the medical bills that they deem "reasonable and customary." Perhaps your insurance company will assert that your ophthalmologist charges more for eye examinations than is normally considered reasonable. In fact, some companies may use dubious methods for arriving at what is a "reasonable" charge, such as using outdated fee schedules or mathematical averages which do not necessarily apply to your case. To avoid being stuck with the bill, write or call the insurance company beforehand to see what the usual charge allowance is for a given procedure. If it is too late and your claim has been adjusted and reduced, but you believe that the charge was in fact "reasonable and customary," you can get estimates from other doctors for the same treatment in order to prove your point, and then pursue it further with the company.

Preexisting Conditions

Preexisting conditions are extremely important to understand in purchasing health insurance. Usually, most applicants have had some preexisting condition. Such preexisting conditions become vitally important when applying for health insurance. If you neglect to disclose a preexisting condition in response to a health insurance application, this could spell trouble for you when you want to collect on a claim. Insurance companies generally check your medical history after a claim is filed, a practice referred to as "post claims underwriting." Insurance companies use this practice to claim that the undisclosed information may have caused them to reject your application when you bought your policy. Your best defense is filling out the application thoroughly, indicating anything that in your judgment might affect the risk of insuring you. The importance of this tip cannot be stressed enough. Your policy is a legally binding contract, and your application becomes part of that contract. Therefore:

It Is Imperative That You Fill Out Your Insurance Application Accurately and Completely Down to the Last Detail, Especially Parts Relating to Medical History. Anything You Do Not State Can and Will Be Used Against You in the World of Insurance. *Your Policy Can Even Be Rescinded.*

The general rule is that when an applicant for insurance is asked material information about his or her health or medical history and does not give the specific information requested or answers untruthfully, the insurance company is entitled to rescind the policy. This means your claim may not be paid, and worse yet, your policy can be canceled. However, not every nondisclosure on an insurance application will provide grounds for rescission. Many times, omissions occur in applications which are trivial or not material. Also, some people just innocently forget about a condition or treatment that occurred sometime in the past. In your case, maybe your allergy has been gone for ten years and did not seem relevant. Accordingly, most courts will not allow an insurance company to rescind if the applicant failed to appreciate the significance of the information when giving an incorrect or incomplete response to a question on an insurance application. Furthermore, questions concerning prior illnesses or diseases must relate to serious ailments rather than just to minor medical problems. Finally, any misrepresentation or omission must be a material one, rather than something insignificant. For example, failing to list a doctor you saw one time for a sprained ankle should not be grounds for rescission when you put in your claim for cancer surgery. In the final analysis, it is important to do the best job you can when filling out an insurance application, trying to be as honest and complete as possible.

Preexisting conditions are also important when it comes to whether or not you have coverage for that condition. You simply must read the policy and ask specific questions concerning coverage for a preexisting condition. Many policies exclude coverage for a preexisting condition while other policies will pay for them if you have been treatment-free for a certain period of time. This becomes critical if you switch policies. You may have coverage for a condition on your old policy which will be excluded as preexisting on a new policy. You must be wary of this potential trap. If you are covered on your present policy, do not switch to a new policy unless you make sure that the condition will also be covered on the new policy.

Finally, you should try to read your policy again when it is time to file a claim. When you do sit down to read it, you will discover that buried in a sea of print is a procedure to be followed for filing a claim. Follow the procedure outlined in the policy and use the forms provided by the company or their agent. You should become familiar with your policy as a starting point. But you also need to become aware of your rights as a consumer and realize that you don't always have to take no for an answer. Yes, insurance companies are equipped with piles of excuses to avoid paying claims, but being informed is the first step toward recovering when an insurance company rejects a claim that seems valid and reasonable to you.

The following section offers a way to avoid another insurance headache—taking precautions to secure your personal property.

V

BEFORE DISASTER STRIKES (PROTECTING YOUR PROPERTY)

Most people have homeowner's insurance policies to protect their home and their valuable possessions. Although your homeowner's policy will cover some personal property losses, you may be required to insure valuables such as antiques, jewelry, furs, works of art, silverware, and camera equipment separately under special riders to your policy. Check with your agent to determine which items are required to be listed separately. As with health insurance, there are certain precautions you can take to maximize your chances of satisfactorily recovering losses. There are also certain conditions that you must satisfy before your claim will be paid. This section will show you how to be prepared for the worst.

Insurance companies rightfully want to avoid giving consumers the idea that they can be as careless as they want with any piece of property that is insured. Therefore, you can avoid problems if you exercise common sense when protecting your insured property by treating it as if it were not insured. Taking care of your possessions is good for you and your insurance company. However, the most important thing you can do to protect your belongings is to:

Take a Detailed Inventory of All Belongings You Insure, Keep Your Inventory Updated, and Keep a Separate Copy Outside of Your Home.

It is very important that you keep good documentation of your possessions and their approximate values, especially since the value of a loss is often difficult to prove. Keep a list of all your major possessions; every time you acquire a new one, log it in. Consumers invariably overlook possessions and forget about them after a flood, tornado, fire, etc. Your inventory will be valuable to you after you have suffered a loss and begin the claim process. Also include the make and model numbers of electronic items such as televisions, computers, microwaves, and stereo equipment.

There are several ways to document your possessions. Sales receipts, photographs, videotapes, and appraisals are all acceptable sources of support, but:

The Best Way to Establish the Original Value of Your Belongings Is with an Original Sales Receipt.

When one is making a claim on lost, stolen, or damaged personal property, sales receipts are invaluable. In some cases they may be required. Stash these receipts in a secure place away from your house, such as a safe-deposit box, where they will be safe in case of a fire or burglary. Of course, it is only human not to keep track of every receipt. If you have lost your receipt, other documents showing proof of purchase should be sufficient, such as canceled checks or credit card statements. Another alternative is to return to the place of purchase after the loss and ask for a duplicate copy of a sales receipt. Most major purchases should still be on record. Appraisals of very expensive items, such as expensive jewelry and artwork, can also be extremely helpful. If you cannot produce anything showing the value of the item, any scrap of evidence verifying your possession of the article is better than nothing. If your Rolex watch was stolen, for example, show your insurance company the box that it came in, the warranty, etc. Even the most heartless thief usually leaves you the box.

It is also a good idea to take pictures of each room to show each of your possessions. Take pictures of possessions such as rugs, antiques, furs, and silverware in order to show their quality and condition. Videotapes are now being used for this purpose as well, which allows you to shoot a room from many angles. Shooting an item from several angles is most important when something has been damaged and you are trying to show the extent of the damage.

Though pictures and videotapes used to be very encouraged by the insurance industry, they may not as helpful as they once were. These days, some claims adjusters say that when someone comes in with a pile of pictures, a red flag goes up in their mind for insurance fraud. The same is true with videotapes. Claims departments continually report cases of fraudulent claims, in which people submit pictures and videos of possessions which are not their own. This is one reason that most claims adjusters prefer sales receipts.

Perhaps now is a good time to take a closer look at these people who evaluate your claim—these claims adjusters. In the next section, we'll discuss what they do, how they operate, and, most importantly, what things are likely to make them pay—or deny—your claim.

VI
WHO HANDLES YOUR CLAIM?

The responsibility for handling your insurance claim gets placed mostly on the shoulders of specialized employees of insurance companies called claims adjusters. It becomes their job to investigate, evaluate, and negotiate your claim. Having a basic understanding of the claims adjusters' approach to handling claims can be helpful when you are depending on them to recover compensation which may well be critical.

Despite the large responsibility they carry, many claims adjusters lack sufficient education, qualifications, and experience. This is because most insurance companies train and pay their sales force better than they do the claims department. After all, the sales force brings in the money and all the claims department does is pay it out. This is no secret. The sales agents get trained well and paid well to do a great job, and claims representatives get the short end of the stick when it comes to pay and training. This is not to say that you can automatically expect a claims adjuster to do a poor job in handling your claim, but to emphasize that claims adjusters are only employees and by no means the utmost authority on every insurance decision. Claims adjusters are ordinary people who can make mistakes. Therefore, if their evaluations appear questionable to you, then you should insist on further review by the insurance company.

The job of a claims adjuster is not always an easy one. They are usually given many claims, or files, to handle simultaneously, and are often under pressure from many sides in processing each claim. The most immediate pressure they encounter is from their supervisors, who, in accordance with protecting the business interests of the insurance company, are going to discourage the overpaying of claims or the paying of exaggerated and illegitimate claims.

Claims adjusters consider it a standard part of the job to counteract fraudulent or exaggerated claims. Most adjusters believe that insurance fraud is rampant and can usually supply you with a large number of insurance fraud "horror stories" if asked. This opinion may cause your adjuster to take a routinely suspicious view of you and your claim. As one ex-adjuster said, "You get to the point where you just don't believe anyone anymore." As a consumer, the best thing that you can do is to dispel these predispositions of an adjuster by not overreaching or exaggerating your claim, and by being as cooperative as possible.

Claims adjusters are likely to be sensitive to customer satisfaction. Like all business people, they will desire to keep a good rapport with you and the rest of their customers, on whose continued business the company depends. Here, it is important to make the distinction between first- and third-party claims. First-party claims are those where your claim is put in with your own company, whereas in third-party claims you are pursuing another person's insurance company. For example, most health, life, and property insurance claims are first-party transactions, in which you are dealing directly with the insurance company as their customer. On the other hand, most auto liability injury claims are third-party transactions, in which you are making a claim against another person's insurance company (that of the person who rear-ended you, for example). Remember,

**In Third-Party Transactions, Such
as Auto Liability Claims, You
Are Not the Customer of the
Insurance Company, and Therefore
an Appearance of Fairness Does
Not Benefit the Future Business
of the Company.**

Hence, third-party claims usually present more of an adversarial climate between you and the insurance company. With this in mind, you might have to stick up for your interests a little more in auto liability claims, since the company will not have the same intrinsic concern with your satisfaction.

One last but very significant pressure that adjusters have in handling insurance claims is the pressure to settle, or to "close the file" and get it off of their desk. In unresolved or dragging cases, adjusters may try especially hard to close the file in order to make one more problem go away. This attitude can work to your disadvantage if the adjuster rejects your claim just to get rid of the file. On the other hand, if you are into negotiations, a persistent attitude on your part may get you a little more money. Having an understanding of these pressures and your adjuster's attitude toward you and your claim helps smooth the way to claim payment.

Remember:

**Insurance Adjusters First Look for
a Reason Not to Pay Your Claim
and, If They Cannot Find One,
Then They Pay It.**

The next chapter is dedicated to filing a claim without giving your insurance company any justification for denying it.

CHAPTER 2

How to File an Airtight Insurance Claim

I
DON'T LEAVE ROOM FOR EXCUSES

Knowing how to file an airtight claim and how to challenge an undesirable settlement offer is your best defense against becoming prey to the abusive practices of insurance companies. Later on, this book tells the stories of consumers who have already become victims, and what they did to combat such abuse. But you can help to guard against another type of abuse in the system—abuse by the consumer. Consumers and lawyers can do more harm than good to a healthy system by making outrageous claims or bringing frivolous lawsuits. Therefore, among the highest recommendations we can make is:

Do Not File False Claims or Overreach by Exaggerating Your Loss. Insurance Fraud Exacerbates Our National Insurance Problems and Is Punishable by Law.

It is not uncommon for people to want more than they deserve. A frequent example is the tendency of people to report old property as if it were new when it becomes damaged. If someone is covered for the current market value of a ten-year-old couch, there is a temptation to claim a brand-new couch, because that is what someone needs to buy in order to replace it. It is precisely this type of thing, particularly the extreme cases, that are used by the insurance industry to make its case for reform of the system. What the insurance industry means by *reform* is usually a *taking away* or *watering down* of our *valuable rights*.

The importance of honesty cannot be overstated. It is a bad idea to inflate your insurance claims for yet another reason. Padded claims can come back to haunt you in one way or another. The most direct impact of an inflated claim may be reflected by the attitude of the claims adjuster. If the claims adjuster thinks the claim is out of line, he or she may take a hostile stance, which will remain throughout the claims process. Once the adjuster gets his or her back up, payment of your claim will probably be very difficult. Indirectly, inflated claims may boomerang and the company may raise your premium. If you exaggerate a claim intentionally, your insurance company may accuse you of insurance fraud, which in most states is a very serious criminal charge.

You should state your losses in a very honest, straightforward, and reasonable fashion. Another way to keep an adjuster from getting his or her back up is to treat him or her with respect. As with all human relations, your attitude is likely to be reflected back on you. If you are respectful and honest, the company has an obligation to process your claim in good faith. It must treat you and your claim in a reasonable fashion—or, as we will see in later chapters—it can be punished.

II
HOW TO PRESENT YOUR PROPERTY LOSSES

When reporting the loss of property, there are certain procedures you can follow that can make your dealings with your insurance company easier for you, as well as increase your chances of getting paid. The following steps are suggested as a general guideline:

Step One: In Cases of Theft, Break-in, Vandalism, or Other Serious Crimes, File a Report with the Police Immediately. Serious Automobile Accidents Should Also Be Reported.

Failure to notify the police after criminal acts have occurred can jeopardize your insurance claim and can even be grounds for denial. Whenever possible, it is desirable to notify the police and have them make a report of the incident. Especially when no witnesses are involved, a police report may be the only tool insurance companies can use for determining the circumstances of the accident, including questions of probable negligence.

Step Two: Take Photographs of Damaged Property Before It Is Repaired and Write Down the Details of the Incident Leading to Your Loss.

Any information you can provide your insurance company detailing your particular situation or indicating the extent of the damages can only help. In traumatic events like thefts or accidents, write down such information as soon as possible so you won't forget. Take pictures of your car or belongings before getting repair work done in order to verify coverage. This way, you can't get stuck with the bill.

Step Three: Notify Your Insurance Company at Once.

It is your responsibility to call your insurance company immediately, notifying them of your loss and asking them to send you a claim form. Promptly complete and return the claim form, sending along the police report, pictures, and other documents, if available.

Step Four: Take the Necessary Measures to Prevent Further Damage to Your Property, or the Insurance Company Can Refuse to Pay for It.

Many policies state that you are responsible for taking precautionary measures to secure your property from further loss or damage. In particular, fix broken locks or windows that can lead to theft and leaks or floods that can further damage your possessions. Call your insurance company and ask them what additional steps you can take toward this end. Insurance companies will normally authorize these types of immediate repairs. If burglars carry off your stereo due to a broken lock, or water from a leaky roof causes the carpet below to mildew, your insurance company does not have to cover the loss. Do not expect to be reimbursed for your personal efforts, however, as most insurers pay only for professional repair people or contractors. Beyond addressing these immediately pressing repairs, you should wait for the insurance company's inspection and authorization before making large, permanent repairs to damaged possessions. In some cases, your company can legally refuse to pay for repairs to items before they are inspected. If your home has been severely damaged, from a fire perhaps, you should try to preserve the remains in an unaltered condition for a reasonable period of time, because your insurance company will want to inspect the premises.

Step Five: Consult Your Insurance Policy for Specific Instructions and to Check Your Coverage.

When you have an insurance claim, check your policy for detailed instructions. Also look it over to verify what is and is not covered. Your coverage may be more extensive than you had thought. For example, one woman was pleasantly surprised to find out that her homeowner's liability insurance paid for an $11,500 vase that she accidentally smashed while browsing in a Mexican antique shop. In another case, a policyholder's homeowner's policy paid the veterinary bill for a neighbor's dog who was bitten by the insured's dog, even though the incident didn't take place at the insured's residence. A homeowner's policy can also cover the repair of a crack in a swimming pool (or floor, ceiling, foundation, etc.) when due to contractor negligence rather than wear and tear. You too might be surprised to find that you have coverages you did not even realize were included in your policy. In summary, anytime you suffer damages in or near your home, look at your homeowner's policy.

Step Six: Fill Out Your Claim Form
Accurately and Completely, and Keep Copies
for Yourself.

Answer all questions on the claim form to the best of your knowledge, indicating how much you are claiming as well as where, when, and how the damage occurred. If you are unable to estimate some part of your claim, such as cleaning and redecorating, notify the insurance company that you plan to make a further claim later. Make sure that your policy number is included with your claim form, and send the paperwork in within 30 days from when you noticed the damage.

This is an important step not only for property claims, but all insurance claims as well. Perhaps one of the greatest reasons for delays or other problems with getting claims paid is that many people do not include the necessary information on the claim form. When you fail to provide sufficient information, the insurance company often has to take extra steps in investigating your claim, and this slows down the whole process. The next step applies to all types of claims as well:

Step Seven: Keep Records of Repair Costs
and Other Losses. Good Documentation Is
Extremely Important.

Keep organized records of all repair work, including copies of contracts with suppliers, workers, and so forth, bills, and receipts. Take notes on why the work was done. It is your job to show the necessity for the services rendered. Therefore, you can request the supporting statements of repair people and contractors. Pictures of your property before and after repairs can also help. If the extent of house repairs forces you to find alternative living accommodations, keep track of all such expenses. Submit all these supporting documents with your claim form.

It is often helpful to include with your claim form a letter that provides a checklist noting all the necessary supporting documents included with the form. Besides supplying all of this documentation, be sure to make and keep copies for yourself (including the claim form). Most people bank on the expectation that they will not encounter any problems recovering reimbursement for their damages and do not make copies for their own records. It is not unusual for documents to get lost or directed to the wrong place, and your duplicate records may be essential to recovering for your loss. It is advisable to wait a reasonable amount of time after mailing in a claim, then to call in with your policy number and ask to speak to a claims adjuster to confirm that your claim form has arrived and has been properly routed to the correct individual.

Step Eight: Send in Your Claim, Attaching Copies of All Necessary Documents.

III
WHAT ARE THE DAMAGES? (ASSESSING YOUR LOSSES AND RESTORING YOUR HOME)

Damage Assessment

Determining the amount and extent of the damages to your property and the cost of repairs can be a long and tiresome business. The usual procedure is for your insurance company to send an insurance adjuster, sometimes called a claims representative, to your house for an on-site inspection and estimation of the damages. He or she will also try to verify that the losses are covered by your policy, that you are the legal owner of the property, and that your address corresponds to the one listed on the policy. As mentioned earlier, you should delay all repairs that aren't essential until this time to make sure they are covered. Don't be in a hurry to clean up before inspection is made; the claims representative may want to take pictures of the damaged condition of goods prior to their repair or replacement.

For the adjuster's benefit as well as your own, extend your full cooperation by supplying any requested information. Tell the adjuster how you can be reached, and keep him or her updated on any new information you find regarding the assessment of damages. If you have any problems dealing with the representative, do not be afraid to contact the adjuster's supervisors or the claims manager. If this does not help, you can file a complaint with your State Department of Insurance. (For the State Department telephone number and address in your state, see Appendix A.)

The wording in your insurance policy may allow for varying interpretations of what you are entitled to. Remember our earlier advice: the adjuster's opinion does not have to be the final judgment if you have a reasonable disagreement with his or her decision.

Though Your Damages May Seem Fairly "Black and White," the Cost of the Repairs May Not Be.

If your opinion is different from the adjuster's, and you are persistent in your contention, your insurance company is likely to offer a compromise rather than to fight it out.

Though the use of insurance adjusters is a traditional method of evaluating losses, there is a recent trend toward self-assessment. The insurance company may simply send you a form on which they ask you to list all of your lost or damaged properties and their approximate values. You may be required to show proof of loss and ownership within sixty days. Though this task is by nature tedious, and the difficulty is compounded by the fact that you have just suffered a loss, there are advantages. In cases of wholesale loss, you are apt to recall possessions overlooked when an adjuster is directing the assessment. You may also find you have a better opportunity to estimate your dollar loss and discover additional ways to document same. You should review your policy and call your insurance company to clarify any uncertainties. If you've recently suffered a loss, try to keep your chin up if possible, and use the preceding suggestions regarding receipts and other documentation. If you are reading this section for purely informational purposes, take this message to heart and begin taking the necessary steps to create or update a list of possessions.

The Public Adjuster

Another option that you have is to hire a professional called a public adjuster who will do this sort of work for a fee. Public adjusters can help you to prepare your claim by interpreting your policy, securing estimates, and taking inventory of your losses. They will also help you to negotiate your insurance settlement—something of interest to them, since they usually take about 10 percent of it. Unlike insurance adjusters, who are paid by insurance companies, public adjusters are commissioned directly by you. Though the standard fee is 10 percent of your recovery, here is something that a public adjuster probably won't tell you:

The Fee of a Public Adjuster Is Negotiable. Some Will Even Work on an Hourly Basis.

Are public adjusters worth it? Public adjusters have fans as well as foes, but many policyholders agree that they may be well worth their fee in certain instances. For example, if your house is totally destroyed, your insurance company is likely to owe you money up to your full policy limits. Here, your recovery is essentially cut-and-dried, so it is unlikely that somebody else can get you more money. However, a public adjuster might be quite useful when your house has been extensively damaged but is not beyond salvation. In this case, a public adjuster might find damage that you are likely to overlook, such as wet insulation behind the walls. A good adjuster might also come up with innovative alternatives for restoration.

Another advantage of hiring a public adjuster is that he or she has usually dealt with insurance companies many times before and understands the way insurance adjusters think. Such knowledge, combined with superior negotiation skills, often adds up to a good chance that a public adjuster can negotiate a better and fairer settlement than you could on your own. Nevertheless, be sure you remember that you are paying a public adjuster and his fee comes out of your settlement.

Representatives of the insurance industry argue that public adjusters needlessly duplicate the work of their own company adjusters and, in the process, inflate the claim by 10 percent in order to make their fee. To insurance companies, it is a counterproductive nuisance for someone to question them over the value of various items. Insurers therefore charge that public adjusters serve to create an adversarial relationship between themselves and their insured.

In the long run, the decision to hire a professional depends on how much you want to free yourself of the headaches of damage assessment and how much larger a settlement you think he or she can secure. For claims below $10,000 and those in which the payment seems fairly black-and-white, it may be well worth it for you to handle the settlement yourself.

You can usually find a public adjuster in the Yellow Pages of your phone book. Before you hire one, however, get some references from several of his or her former clients, ask to see his or her license, and check to see if he or she is a member of the National Association of Public Insurance Adjusters. Public adjusters can abuse their authority, so exercise some caution. The last thing you need is another insurance-related problem.

Hiring a Contractor

If damage to your home is extensive, you will probably need to hire a contractor to do repair work. Depending on the circumstances, you may want to consider hiring a fire- or water-damage restoration contractor. As opposed to general contractors, restoration contractors specialize in repair work involving fire and water damage, such as removing the smoke residue from your furniture and air-conditioning ducts, or removing water from flooded carpets or flooring. In addition, restoration contractors normally are trained to perform services that meet insurance contract requirements—for example, providing emergency services and protecting your property from further damage. This can include anything from boarding up windows to repairing the roof to drying out your home. They can also help you to obtain the necessary estimates to evaluate the scope of your loss, and to make sure that repair work is done in accordance with the estimates.

Insurance companies normally have their own contractors that they recommend. These contractors will usually do the job relatively cheaply in return for getting a large volume of the insurance companies' business. Obtain estimates from independent contractors first, and then compare these with those of the company's contractor. Where there are major discrepancies in cost or materials, discuss these with both contractors to determine why and what is necessary to secure your satisfaction and to avoid costly repairs in the future. The fact that the insurance company's contractor saves money doesn't mean there is anything wrong with using him or her, but:

If You Use a Contractor Provided by Your Insurance Company, Make Sure to Get a Guarantee of Quality from the Contractor and Your Insurance Adjuster. Otherwise, Get Your Own Contractor.

Have both your insurer's contractor and your insurance adjuster sign statements guaranteeing that the job will be done "in a satisfactory manner and to the acceptable standards of the construction industry." When their contractor says he will do a "cheap" job, you want to be sure he is referring to expense but not quality. In cases where there is a significant difference between the estimate of repairs from the insurance company's contractor and the one you have selected, most policies provide for an umpire to settle this difference. You can invoke this remedy simply by requesting this procedure to resolve the conflict between the two estimates.

If you are forced into temporary housing and eating out while repair work is being done on your home, your insurance company will usually reimburse you for the difference between these expenses and your normal living expenses, up to the limits stated in the policy. It is best to get approval in writing from your insurance adjuster, however, and to establish in advance where you will be staying. Most problems with reimbursements of this kind are simply due to a lack of this type of communication. Keep in mind that your policy limit for additional living expenses is a fixed amount regardless of the period of time you need alternative accommodations. This means that if you are allotted $1,000 for such expenses under the terms of your policy, you could afford to check into a very nice hotel if repairs will only take a couple of days, but not if they take a couple of weeks. Once your fixed amount has been exhausted, you will be responsible for the remainder of the costs.

It goes without saying that a disaster occurring to an individual's house is probably one of the worst experiences anyone can undergo, especially if people are hurt in the process. With any luck, karma, or help from God, you won't be plagued by such misfortune. But if you are, you can definitely do without major hassles or problems with insurance. We hope that the preceding comments will help prevent a major loss from becoming a twofold calamity. Now we turn to helping you to prepare your insurance claim in case of another tragic event—an automobile accident.

IV
WHAT TO DO IF YOU ARE IN A CAR ACCIDENT

Car accidents are no laughing matter. If you have ever been in one—and most people have at one time or another—you know what a pain they can be, even if you haven't been hurt physically. Whether a car was "totaled" or a fender was bent, insurance can play a role in resolving the inevitable problems arising from injuries to persons and property, and potential litigation. Following the steps below can help to alleviate some of the paperwork drudgery, reduce anxiety, and maximize your chances of a satisfactory outcome when filing a claim with your own insurance company or against another driver's.

Step One: Check for Injuries and Call for Emergency Services if Necessary.

If you are involved in an accident, and there are injuries, call for an ambulance or the paramedics immediately.

Step Two: Call the Police.

Always call the police if someone has been hurt. Even if nobody seems injured, it is a good idea to call the police, as most state laws require notifying the police when the damage to the vehicle exceeds some fixed amount like $300.

By law, the police must file a formal report. Therefore, you may be legally obligated to report even small fender-benders, if the cost of repairs is over the state's dollar limit. Unless the accident occurs on a state highway, the city or county police department usually has jurisdiction over these matters.

For insurance purposes, it is always a good idea to have a police report filed, as it will assist in the handling of your claim. In fact, you hurt your chances of getting your claim paid if there is no police report. Depending on the seriousness and the location of the accident, the police may not come to the scene, but you should always make the attempt, except for very minor incidents. Even if the police will not respond, they will usually document your attempt to report the accident, which could prove helpful later on in the claims process.

Step Three: Gather Necessary Information from Other People. This Includes Identifying Information of Drivers, Passengers, and Especially Witnesses. Trade Insurance Information with Other Drivers as Well.

First, exchange names, addresses, telephone numbers, and license numbers with all other drivers involved. Also get license plate and vehicle registration numbers, along with the year and make, of the cars involved. Check to see if the name and other information on the registration correspond to those on the license. Ask questions and make notes if they do not. Perhaps the car is owned by someone other than the actual driver—this is good to know. Most importantly, exchange the name, address, and telephone numbers of your insurance companies, as well as policy numbers. If the owner of a damaged car cannot be found (for example, if you have hit a parked car), leave a note with the identifying information of all the drivers and owners involved.

Make sure to get the name, address, and number of other passengers and any possible witnesses. According to one claims manager, forgetting to do this is the biggest mistake people make in filing auto insurance claims. Insurance companies need to substantiate your claim, and a police report is not always sufficient. Therefore, you should actively seek out witnesses instead of waiting for them to come to you. Witnesses who can verify that the other driver was at fault (for example, if the other driver ran a stop sign) may be critical to you. Get their name, address, and phone number, and encourage them to make a statement to the police officer investigating the accident. If you are a witness to an accident, your assistance will be highly appreciated. Many people are afraid to "get involved" by giving their name if they are witness to

an accident, but claims representatives point out that witnesses usually help to resolve a case immediately; it is mostly
accidents without witnesses in which disputes arise.

Step Four: Gather Evidence Describing the Accident.

Details are important for insurance claims. Unless a serious
traffic hazard might result, you should leave all involved cars
in their final position after the collision. Establishing the
stopping place of the cars can be important in determining
the facts of the accident. If you have a camera, take photographs of the positions of all cars involved and any damage
sustained by the vehicles. If you don't have a camera, draw-
ing a simple diagram can also be useful, especially in cases
where the police are delayed or will not respond.

Skid marks can be a valuable bit of evidence as well.
Inspect the direction and length of such marks and mark them
on your diagram. Skid marks can often indicate the speed of
the car at the time of the accident and are therefore useful in
establishing fault. Also note the impact marks on the road-
way, dividers, and other vehicles. The police should make a
more detailed diagram of the accident, but it certainly
wouldn't hurt to make one for yourself if the circumstances
warrant this effort.

Step Five: Do Not Sign Any Statements or Documents Other Than the Police Report.

Don't sign or make statements indicating that you are at fault,
that you will pay for damages, or that you are willing to forget
about the accident. Nor should you sign any sort of promise
releasing other parties from further responsibility. If you do,

an insurance company may refuse to pay for damage to your car or you could be hurting your chances of collecting on an injury claim. It is best to let the responsibilities of the parties be determined later or when all the evidence has been gathered. Foolish or inaccurate statements at the scene of an accident can come back to haunt you.

Step Six: Notify Your Insurance Company Immediately.

As a policyholder, it is *your* responsibility to do so. Delays in notifying your insurer could affect the way your claim is handled. Once your filing is a matter of record, someone from the claims department should contact you within a short period—usually one to three days. If you do not hear from anyone within this time, call your insurance company for assistance. If your company is still unresponsive, contact your State Department of Insurance. (See Chapter 3.)

Step Seven: Notify the Department of Motor Vehicles.

The same rule applies for notifying your State Department of Motor Vehicles as notifying the police. You must advise the DMV of accidents involving injury or where damages to your vehicle exceed a fixed amount ($500 in California, for example). Failure to do so *within 10 days* of the accident can result in the *suspension of your driver's license.*

Step Eight: Delay Repairs Until an Insurance Adjuster's Inspection Is Completed. Offer Your Cooperation to the Adjuster to Aid His or Her Investigation.

An adjuster or appraiser will usually be sent to inspect your vehicle if it has been badly damaged. Provide him or her with any necessary information. Your insurance company may request that you obtain several written estimates from repair shops before authorizing that the work be done. Some companies may direct you to their own repair shop. You have the right to make sure that—whatever repair shop is selected—you are satisfied with the quality of their work and the extent of repairs that have been approved.

If you are unhappy about the repair work done, notify your insurance company and insist that corrections be made, until you are satisfied. If a dispute arises, see Chapter 3 on challenging insurance company rulings.

Step Nine: Obtain Estimates on the Value of Your Claim.

Consumer-education efforts have now impressed on drivers the importance of obtaining pictures and estimates of damage to automobiles. As with any documentation, however, you should not send originals of a photograph without keeping a copy for yourself. The same thing holds for repair estimates, service-station receipts, towing-service charges, and bills for repairs already made. Disputes over the value of a car involved in a theft or an accident are fairly common. Service receipts, a repair history, maintenance history, and mileage are all invaluable when you are trying to establish the condition of your car after it has been lost or destroyed. In addition to the particular condition of your own car, there are general guidelines for the value of each make and model. If your insurance company makes an estimate of repair costs based on evaluations by a repair shop that you think does shoddy work, challenge their estimate by getting a few of your own estimates from shops of your choice.

Make sure you are getting fair value for your car if the company wants to write it off or "total" it. Most insurance companies will offer you the actual cash value (ACV) of your car before the accident. This is a price that a buyer would have paid for your car had it not been destroyed, factoring in the year, make, mileage, and previous damage. To estimate the ACV of your car, your company may survey used car dealers or other sellers, use value guide books, or employ computerized market analysis.

If you do not agree with your insurer's assessment of the ACV, make your own investigation. You too can survey car dealers or private sellers. Another way to determine a fair cash value is to check the amount against the value listed in *The Kelley Blue Book* (commonly called "The Blue Book"). This book is used throughout the auto industry to establish the value of used cars. It is published by the Kelley Blue Book Company, 5 Oldfield, Irvine, CA 92718, (714) 770-7704; anyone can purchase one. It is also widely available through libraries. This book provides a wealth of information concerning the value of your car. Since these are the values that are generally accepted in the auto industry, it may be unfair for an insurance company to offer you anything less.

A word of caution: remember that the value of your car may be *higher* than the value indicated in *The Kelley Blue Book* or other car guides if your car has low mileage or if you have records of recent improvements to your car, such as a new paint job. You may add the cost of such improvements to the value in the guide. Your insurance company could give you a lowball estimate if you do not provide them with such relevant information. Insurance companies must consider all information you present them. So if you can demonstrate convincingly that your higher valuation more accurately reflects the ACV of your car, they should be willing to negotiate. If they ignore such pertinent information, you have good reason to challenge them.

Step Ten: File Your Claim Promptly and Document It Thoroughly.

Make sure to attach all receipts, photographs, and other supporting documentation to your claim form.

Compensation

The amount of your recovery will depend on the total repair costs as well as your contribution of fault—the percentage of an accident that the authorities say you are responsible for—and the laws governing your state. Many states, such as California, use a comparative negligence system. Under the comparative negligence rule, if you are found to be partially at fault in the accident, the insurance company will reduce your payment by the percentage of your fault. We'll use an example to make this clear.

Let's say the insurance company maintains an accident was 20 percent your fault. You would only recover $8,000 of your $10,000 claim. If you are only 5 percent at fault and the other driver is 95 percent at fault, you would recover $9,500—almost your full claim.

Most states have converted to this comparative negligence rule from a former rule of contributory negligence. Some states have not converted, however, and still favor contributory negligence. Under contributory negligence, if you are found to have contributed to the cause of the accident at all, you can be ineligible to recover any part of your claim. In the above example, the insurance company would not have to pay your claim even if you were determined to be only 5 percent at fault. Somehow it doesn't seem quite fair not to be compensated for being hit by someone who is found to be 95 percent responsible for the accident. However, most claimants found to be only partially at fault in states using contributory negligence usually do receive some form of compensation in practice. If you feel that you are a victim of this rule, appeal the insurance company's decision and obtain a lawyer if necessary. The inherent unfairness of the contributory negligence policy explains why most states have changed to a system based on comparative negligence.

Both comparative and contributory negligence systems of determining liability require you to file your claim with the other driver's insurance company; that is, all of these claims are made by you against a third party's (other driver's) insurance company, other than your own insurance company. Some states now use a system of no-fault liability insurance, in which you are reimbursed by your own insurance company without regard to fault. To determine what liability laws apply in your state, contact your State Department of Insurance. (See Chapter 3.)

Also, if you have "collision" coverage on your own automobile insurance policy, you may want to put in a claim for your vehicle damage with your company. Your carrier, after paying you, will then go after the guilty party's carrier for reimbursement. In many cases, this is the fastest way to go because the concept of no fault does not affect your collision coverage. Accordingly, you may end up recovering your car damages from your own insurance carrier if the third party's insurance company does not pay or is being too slow (over a month or two) or wants to reduce your claim due to the fault concept. The one drawback to collecting from your carrier rather than the other person's carrier is that your rates could go up.

Of course, you may have other significant damages from a car accident, like loss of earnings and physical injury claims. Unless the injury is slight, it is best to get the advice of a lawyer before finally settling these claims, as the variables are too complex to reduce to basic rules.

V

TIPS ON HEALTH INSURANCE

Next we look at some practical tips for filing health insurance claims. Because of the tens of millions of medical insurance claims filed every year, this is one line of insurance in which you are most likely to confront difficulties. Here are some tips with regard to several aspects of health insurance claims.

Claim Forms

Sometimes medical claims are complicated because several parties must participate in processing the claim form. Typically, the policyholder obtains a copy of a claim form from his or her employer or group policyholder. The person then fills out the individual policyholder's portion and gives the form to the doctor who performed the services or prescribed medication or treatments. The doctor must fill out the "attending physician's" part of the form and send the form to the insurance carrier or return it to the policyholder. The potential problems that can arise at any stage are usually the result of the policyholder's failing to complete the form properly. Stumbling blocks to speedy reimbursement may range from something as simple as failing to include the date you visited the doctor to something as complicated as inadequately explaining why the doctor had to perform additional surgery resulting from complications arising out of the initial procedure, i.e., in the first round of treatments or surgery. If your insurance company says it needs more medical information, you must get to the bottom of the problem *immediately.*

Discuss the Situation with Your Doctor's Office and Get the Doctor Involved. Ask the Doctor's Office to Help You by Providing You with Detailed Information and Explanations, Then Supply the Company with This Documentation Yourself.

Many times you will discover that further clarification from the doctor's office will be sufficient to convince a hesitant insurance company to reimburse you. In this case, you should make an effort to have an additional supporting communication from the doctor's office sent to your insurer. Keep a copy in your file. In a week or so, check with your doctor to make sure that he or she has sent the appropriate materials, or with your insurance company to verify that they have been received. Often, people assume that their insurance company is delaying its response when, in reality, their claim has not been fully processed because supporting documents have not yet been received by the claims department.

The "Two Opinion" Requirement

Most insurance companies will pay for a second opinion, especially if surgery is recommended, and some actually *require* that you obtain a second opinion in order to receive full benefits. Therefore, if surgery is required, make sure you get a second opinion.

Precertification

Some insurance companies require that you "precertify" your doctor bills by calling in before your visit to the doctor and confirming that the treatment is covered. Usually a toll-free "800" number is provided to policyholders for this purpose. Such insurers will be much less likely to hassle you over a bill—to claim, for example, that it is "unreasonable"—if you call first to precertify your treatment.

Deductibles

Almost all medical health insurance plans come with deductibles. What this means is that, every year, the health insurance plan will pay for all or part of your medical expenses beyond a certain fixed amount, perhaps $100 or $200. If you have a medical bill early in the calendar year and you haven't met your deductible yet, you have to pay for it yourself—up to your deductible limit. Therefore, if your bill is for $250, and your deductible is $200, you can claim only $50 and hope to be reimbursed for whatever percentage of the $50 your policy will pay. However, you may subsequently claim the full amount of each following bill through the calendar year. Since in effect there is no insurance coverage until the top of the deductible limit has been reached, many people don't submit early bills to their health insurance company—especially small ones. To get more for your insurance dollar, however, it would be smart to submit those bills, too, so that they apply against your deductible. If you incur a large medical expense later in the year, from a serious injury perhaps, your earlier bills will have met or nearly met your deductible, and you should receive full coverage, or close to the full coverage, on your injury.

You can also schedule your medical treatments in such a

way that you can collect the maximum allowable amount of reimbursement. For example, if you know you need to have your tonsils removed but have been waiting for the "right time," your insurance deductible can help decide when that might be. Assuming your deductible has been met, it would be best to get your tonsils removed before the end of the year. If you wait until next year, you will also have to wait until your deductible is met again before you can be reimbursed.

Group Health Insurance

Many people have "group health" insurance. This means that the insurance is purchased through their place of employment or some group they belong to, such as a club or association. The group (employer or association) will receive the master insurance policy, and you, as the employee or club member, may get only a descriptive booklet outlining the coverage.

In Group Policies, the Descriptive Booklet Outlining the Coverage Is Essential Reading.

If you are involved in such a policy, *be sure you save the booklet,* as this generally outlines the coverages and exclusions in simple terms and gives the insured detailed instructions on how to file a claim. It also generally contains information on how to appeal an adverse claim ruling. Due to the fact that most group health policies are obtained through employment, most employers have special medical insurance administrators to help you with questions concerning coverage and claim filings. You should not hesitate to contact that person if you have any questions or problems.

For examples of policyholders who contested denials of medical claims and won their claims plus damages, see Chapters 6, 7, and 8.

If your group insurance policy is terminated because you are leaving your current place of employment or for any other reason, you may consider getting a conversion policy. Conversion policies "convert" your old group insurance to individual health insurance, in which you are the sole payer of premiums as well as recipient of benefits. Conversion policies, sometimes nicknamed "bare-bones" policies, are generally less desirable than the group policy because they cost more to maintain and because they may drastically reduce your coverage "down to the bone." Nevertheless, conversion policies may still be better than individual health insurance policies that cost so much that they may be out of reach to the average consumer.

Additionally, under a federal law known as COBRA (Consolidated Omnibus Budget Reconciliation Act), you may be entitled to stay on the group plan for up to one and a half years, and your dependents may stay on the plan for up to three years, by electing to do so and paying the premiums. Accordingly, it is very important, upon leaving employment or any other type of group insurance termination, to check your rights under COBRA. It is mandatory that your employer or group carrier fully inform you of these vital rights—so be sure to ask.

Lastly, if you are being treated for a specific illness or accident during termination of the group policy, your benefits may be extended beyond termination under some circumstances. The area of "extension of benefits" for people "on claim" is somewhat controversial and it is probably best to seek legal advice if a problem arises over continued benefits.

VI
DISABILITY AND LIFE INSURANCE CLAIMS

Disability Insurance Claims

Disability insurance claims are often confusing because state laws may define disability in one way, while an insurance company defines it in another way. Insurance companies sell policies nationwide with uniform descriptions of "disability," even though this definition is not always valid under the laws of every state. In California, for example, people are considered totally disabled if they are unable to work *with reasonable continuity*—i.e., steadily—in their customary occupation or in any other occupation in which they might reasonably be expected to engage, considering the opportunities of the job market and their past employment, education, and physical and mental capacity. For example, a truck driver who has a bad back may meet this test of disability if he is not suited for any other work by education, training, or experience and cannot drive a truck because of his bad back. (See Chapter 10 for an example of a case involving this issue.) Even so, many insurance companies sell disability coverage in California, for example, using a definition of "disability" which says that people are disabled only if they are unable to engage in any occupation or employment at any level. In order to avoid falling victim to this overly broad definition,

Be Sure That Your Doctor Fully Understands Your Job Description, Your Employment History, and Your Education Before He or She Evaluates Whether, Considering Your Physical Condition, You Reasonably May Be Expected to Work.

What this means is that you must inform your doctor of the nature of your injury and precisely how it affects your ability to work. The doctor will report your condition to the insurance carrier and must know the extent of your past experience, training, and education in order to determine if you can work at some other job.

If you are denied a claim under a disability policy, make sure the company is acting properly. Sometimes, as pointed out, they may be using an erroneous definition of "disability." Also, some companies have been known to use their own doctors to give conflicting medical reports. You may be entitled to years of future benefits, and a little checking and protesting may prove very beneficial. Getting your treating doctor to support your claim is very helpful. (See Chapters 5 and 10 for good examples of insureds who fought and won their disability claims.)

Life Insurance Claims

Unlike with disability, we usually know when somebody is dead. You don't have to worry too much about an insurance company's telling you that your uncle Rudy is technically not dead after he is six feet underground—although one sometimes suspects even this wouldn't be a complete surprise in the insurance industry.

In life insurance claims, one of the biggest problems is

identifying the proper beneficiary. Many times, someone will designate one of his beneficiaries as "my wife." This can be a problem for someone who has been married several times. The next thing you know, four ex-wives are calling the insurance company, saying, "I'm the only one he really loved." The same thing applies for people naming their "aunt" or "grandfather" as beneficiaries. The best thing you can do to avoid this type of a problem is to:

Be Specific on Your Beneficiary Statement.

In other words, make sure the proper name and relationship of the beneficiary is clearly stated. If you switch to a new policy or get increased coverage, make sure that you fill out a new beneficiary statement, naming specific beneficiaries.

If these precautions have not been taken, however, and you—as a potential beneficiary of a life insurance policy— are involved in this type of dispute, it is best to be up-front and to tell the insurance company everything you know, including the whereabouts of competing beneficiaries. While you might be tempted to try to hide such information, especially if you think it can jeopardize your claim, just remember: so doing only slows the investigative process of the insurance company and delays all payouts. If the insurance company cannot make a decision based on the information they have, they will send the case to court for a judge to make the allocations.

Another mistake people make with life insurance claims is simply not following claims procedures or not providing enough information. Along with the claim form, you should send in your identifying information, such as a marriage or birth certificate, your policy number (a certified copy of the policy is not necessary), the name of the deceased, and a certified death certificate (not a copy). Again, copy all of these documents before sending them. As with all claims, it is also a good practice to keep a running list showing all of your actions involving the claim, including names of persons contacted, dates, and a thumbnail description of what was discussed and any promises or guarantees made.

Occasionally, serious disputes can arise over double-indemnity provisions (in which the policy pays double for *accidental* death) or whether a death is caused by suicide. Many such disputes end up in court. See Chapter 12 for a good example of an interesting claim by a widow under a life policy who refused to believe her husband committed suicide, as the insurance company contended.

VII
NEGOTIATION TACTICS

The vast majority of all claims presented to insurance companies are indeed paid. Most cases are settled through the process of negotiation between the insurance adjuster and the claimant. In fact, more than 19 out of 20 cases are closed through negotiations without legal representation. Chances are, your claim will be resolved through this process as well.

Understandably, most claimants are not trained as skilled negotiators. There is a tendency for them to be naive or unassertive when they negotiate. This does not have to be the case, however. Where the ignorant claimant is penalized for his ignorance, the sophisticated claimant is rewarded for his sophistication. Remember, a well-negotiated settlement is always a good solution. The advantages of a settlement reached through negotiation—not litigation—are considerable in terms of time and money to both you and the insurance company. Here are some tips that can help you in your negotiation.

1. Compromise Is Everything

Compromise is the key to most successful negotiations. You should have a sense of when to compromise, how much to compromise, and how to get the insurance company to compromise. A skilled negotiator will be able to get both sides to withdraw from their initial demands in favor of an acceptable alternative. If you think you have a valid claim, you should not have to do all of the compromising. On the other hand, you should not hold so firmly to your demand that there is no room to make progress through negotiation.

Concessions on one side are generally met with concessions on the other. The amount of the concessions is another issue. Obviously, it is advantageous to give on a smaller scale than you take. One side may make a more extreme initial demand, but is willing to come down (or go up) more. Try to balance the concessions that are made, even if they are not for similar amounts. If your insurance company raises its most recent offer, it is usually a good idea to compromise your demand, as long as your new demand is still satisfactory. A reciprocated concession is a sign of cooperation, and an unreciprocated concession can be viewed as an invitation to trial. On the other hand, avoid making two concessions in a row, as this can be interpreted as a sign of weakness.

Bargain in good faith, and expect the same from your insurance company. A good faith negotiator is willing to reach an agreement and to follow standard rules of procedure to obtain one. A bad faith negotiator uses the process of exchanging proposals to gain more time, information, etc., in order to undercut the case of the opposing side. Watch out for such tactics. Insurance companies have been known to create fictitious disputes (like insinuating you set fire to your house) in order to scare you into an unreasonable compromise. Don't accept these types of games from your insurance company. Insist on fair and reasonable offers.

2. Facts Are Everything

Stick to the facts; they are the most powerful tool you have. Try to leave emotions and other intangibles out of the negotiation. Bringing emotional issues to the forefront of your argument is unlikely to help you and only serves to push your valuable facts to the background.

It is best to be friendly, respectful, and constructive. A positive approach usually leads to positive results. Orient all of your energy toward solving the problem rather than placing blame. Listen carefully to your insurance company's presentation, make an effort to understand their perspective, ask pertinent questions to make sure you understand clearly, and restate the insurance company representative's argument to signify that you understand. Take notes for your own reference. Then state your position, reinterpreting all of the facts as you see them, consulting your notes as need be. Do not be shy or timid in stating your case; present your position clearly and forcefully; remember: a little charisma can do wonders. Try to expose any weaknesses in the insurance company's position. Whatever you do, act professionally and you will be treated with more respect in the long run.

3. Timing Is Everything

There is a time to initiate negotiation and a time to walk away; there is a time to yield and a time to hold strong. Having a good sense of timing can work miracles, just as bad timing can undo them. A reasonable demand or concession at the wrong time can have adverse effects on your settlement. Responding to an offer too quickly can be interpreted as overeagerness.

Similarly, there is a time to say "no." Don't be afraid to refuse an offer if it does not seem reasonable to you. Hearing you say "no" makes your insurance company aware that you know where to draw the line, that you have the courage to stand firm for what you feel is rightfully due you, and that you have the patience to prolong negotiations if need be.

4. Satisfaction Is Everything

Do not sign a settlement agreement until you are satisfied. If your claim is legitimate, you should not settle for less than the minimum compensation that you deserve. Most insurance adjusters realize that you have a lower limit—the least possible amount you can manage with. Anything less is simply unacceptable. This "bottom line" may involve factors beyond a simple tallying up of bills. If you have been injured in some sort of accident, for example, you may feel that you deserve more than just your doctor bills and other expenses.

Though you should not accept final payment until your case is resolved satisfactorily, there is no harm in accepting partial payments in order to pay for bills, repairs, and other expenses, as long as your insurance company formally acknowledges that it is only a partial payment. If you can't get any satisfaction through negotiation, however, it is time for you to take further measures to challenge your insurance company's decision. This subject will be the focus of the next chapter.

CHAPTER 3

How to Challenge an Insurance Ruling

Step 1: Know That You Can Contest an Unfair Decision.

Several years ago, Judith Haut underwent an emergency Caesarean section operation in order to give birth to her son Bryan. As if the childbirth were not struggle enough, next came problems with her insurance company—which paid $500 less than she expected. The reason given: that her doctor charged too much based on average costs for such an operation within her particular geographic area. "I got so angry that I called every OB/GYN in the Santa Monica Yellow Pages and asked what they charged for C-sections," remembers Haut.

She called a total of 27 doctors' offices to discover that only three charged less than her OB/GYN and ten charged more. Her husband, a lawyer, wrote a letter to the insurance company stating that his wife's doctor's fees were clearly "reasonable and customary," based on her research. The insurance company had to agree and paid up.

Haut and the rest of the consumers mentioned in this book are among the select few who have learned to fight back.

Surveys have found that an alarmingly small proportion of people with insurance claims question claim denials—fewer than 1 percent. This number is surprisingly low, considering that as many as 10 percent of all claims may be unjustly rejected. The good news is that, of those who do contest a denial, a majority win their case or improve their position. If need be, you too can fight back—and win.

If you think that your insurance company has denied your claim wrongfully, speak up and be mentally prepared for what is going to happen next. Statistically, insurance companies count on the fact that most people will accept their decisions and will be unwilling or unable to protest. This is usually the last the company ever hears from the policy-holder. Do not assume that the first "no" you receive is the final answer. Do not always accept everything your claims adjuster tells you at face value, either.

You might want to keep some of Grandmother's old adages in mind if you are faced with a negative insurance ruling. These provide a concise formula for challenging such a denial:

1. DON'T PUT OFF UNTIL TOMORROW WHAT YOU CAN DO TODAY
2. A SQUEAKY WHEEL GETS THE GREASE
3. HONESTY IS THE BEST POLICY
4. YOU CAN CATCH MORE FLIES WITH HONEY THAN WITH VINEGAR

Grandmother can't tell you everything, however. The following is a more detailed set of instructions that you can use as a guide if you believe your insurer's decision was unfair.

Step 2: Insist on a Written Explanation.

Many times an insurance claim may be denied without an adequate explanation. Don't settle for this.

Always Get an Explanation in Writing. Most State Laws Require an Insurance Company to Provide You with a Written Explanation When a Claim Is Denied. The Company's Failure to Do This May Be an Unfair Claims Practice.

Step 3: Consider What *You* Think.

Once you receive the company's written explanation for the denial of your claim, read your policy again. You may well find that, though the company is reading the same words you are, they have come up with a very different interpretation— almost as though the meanings come from widely differing dictionaries. With the policy knowledge you have already gained, you know that language will be interpreted as a layperson would understand it. Also, policy provisions will be given their most reasonable interpretation based on the expectations of the policyholder. In short, make sure that the reason for the denial of your claim is legitimate. This may be difficult to do at the outset. You must rely on your own sense for "what is fair" and "what you expected." If it doesn't sound fair, there is a good chance that it isn't. If you have any question or suspicion, you ought to continue following up on the matter until your doubts have been laid to rest.

Remember that your rights are governed by the words and phrases in the insurance policy. Interpretation and meaning of the language will be critical to you. You should carefully read the explanations provided to you. If there is a dispute over your coverage, your interpretation may well be given preference over and above the insurance company's explanation of what those words mean. Many times various words are actually defined in the insurance policy. However, more often than not, certain key words or phrases are not explained. For example, what does "custodial care" mean in a health policy, or what is covered under "skilled nursing care"? See Chapter 9 for a good example of this problem. Insurance companies use such vague, undefined terms to exclude coverage. But you should know that where language is vague, you have a good case. Probably the best general guideline to follow is this:

Take the Insurance Company's Explanation for Denial and Test It by Reading Your Own Policy and Determining for Yourself if the Explanation Is Satisfactory to You. If It Is Not, Pursue the Matter Further.

One example of an unsatisfactory explanation may be the denial of your claim because there was a technical problem with how you filled out or when you filed your claim form. Most insurance policies spell out the company's requirements for filling out the claims forms, including specified time limits (usually 30 days) in which certain forms have to be sent to the company. It would be a good idea to follow these steps religiously. But if you forget to dot the "i" or cross the "t," or if you are late in getting the forms to the company—even months late—don't think all is doomed. If the company denies your claim because of some deficiency in filling out the forms or in getting them in on time, write them back and remind them of this rule that has been universally handed down by courts:

Failure to Properly Fill Out Insurance Forms or Get Them in to the Company on Time Is of No Consequence to an Otherwise Valid Claim, Unless the Insurance Company Can Show It Has Been Harmed by This Failure.

This means that the insurance company has the burden of showing that a deficiency in the claims procedure prevented it from carrying out an adequate investigation or otherwise hurt its ability to handle the claim properly. In most cases, technical deficiencies will not cause an insurance company any problems and should not be used as a reason to deny a claim. Of course, it is always best to file the claim properly, quickly, and in the company's expected format. This helps assure that the company will be less likely to engage in foot dragging or other delaying tactics, and you will get your claim paid faster. *Never consciously delay filing a claim because of this rule:* but regard it as "backup" help if circumstances or misreading instructions result in your claim being filed late or incorrectly filled out.

Step 4: Enlist the Support of Your Insurance Agent.

If you are having trouble getting your claim paid, contact the agent who sold you the policy. Provide your agent with your policy number and a description of the problem. This can be done over the phone but it is best to follow up with a confirming letter stating the problem and requesting an answer. Insurance agents portray themselves as knowledgeable in obtaining coverage for your specific needs. This knowledge creates a duty on their part to find and sell you the kind of coverage you require. Therefore:

The Agent Who Sold You the Policy Has a Duty to Obtain the Correct Coverage for You and to Protect Your Interests.

Often your agent will go to bat for you by contacting the company's claims department on your behalf. This is particularly true with homeowner and automobile insurance claims, since your agent knows you personally and has received a commission for selling the policy to you. In order to keep your business and his or her reputation, your agent may be willing to act as an intermediary between you and the company. If you have a group policy, there may be an administrator appointed to handle claims from your employer or group. This person usually knows about that particular policy and the claims-processing procedure of that insurance company. Many times a little nudge from these intermediaries is all that is needed.

Step 5: Voice Your Complaint to Your Insurance Company.

If a phone call or letter to your insurance agent doesn't solve the problem within a reasonable time, like 30 days, then it's time for direct contact with your insurance company's claims department. It is important to be persistent and:

If You Are Not Satisfied by Personnel at the Level You Are Dealing With, Keep Going Up the Ladder.

Many problems that people have with insurance companies are due primarily to a lack of communication. At the initial stages, a telephone call may clear up misunderstandings or accidental claims mishandlings. There are simple ways to make telephone calls efficiently and to document the substance of the conversation. Have all your papers—your policy, the claim form, the related bills—close at hand when you make the telephone call. *Save your telephone bills* because a serious insurance problem may require long-distance telephone calls, and phone bills will prove the call was made and the exact date you spoke to the company.

Always ask for the identity of the person to whom you are speaking and whether he or she has the authority to handle your questions. Getting a name can help because it may make the insurance representative feel personally accountable for your complaint. Besides the name, keep a telephone log of the dates, times, and telephone numbers. Follow up your conversation with a brief letter to that person stating your understanding of the call, and ask him or her to respond by a certain date if your understanding is incorrect. Even if you are unable to obtain any information of substance, enter into your telephone log what transpired during the conversation.

It is important to keep good records because they may eventually support you in any dispute over how your claim was handled. "Be sure you document whom you spoke to and when you talked. And take notes on what was said," advises Robert Hunter, president of the National Insurance Consumer Organization. "It's a little extra work, but it's worth it in the end. It can make all the difference in the world in settling a claim."

Step 6: Put Your Complaint in Writing.

If you find that you have made several phone calls, and you still feel that you are not making any progress, it is time to state your complaint in writing. Start with the person who denied your claim. This person may be the least likely to change his or her mind, however, so repeated appeals to him or her may be like beating a dead horse. If you cannot resolve matters on this level, you should then write to that person's supervisor or manager: in other words, if you are unable to obtain satisfaction at the level at which you are communicating, try to find out who is at a higher level in the company and communicate with that person. If you cannot discover that person's name, simply address your letter to "claims supervisor" or "claims manager." Most companies have claims managers, supervisors, or even consumer complaint departments that will get involved in problem claims and give them special attention. If you have a real gripe and want to reach the top, you may obtain the name and address of the president of each company from the A. M. Best Company's *Rating Book of Insurance Companies,* which is available in most libraries or can be obtained directly (see Chapter 1).

When you write to your insurance company:

(1) Tell them your policy number and explain your concern rationally and clearly. Make sure to explain the real life effects that their decision is having on you. If you just had heart surgery and are afraid to go to the doctor because your medical bills are not being paid, include this information. Always relate your story courteously and respectfully rather than emotionally, however. "Just the facts, ma'am (or sir)" is a good rule of thumb.

(2) Enclose copies of all relevant information, such as your claim forms, the bills or invoices for which you are claiming coverage, supporting documents, etc.

(3) Insist that the company make a written response to your inquiry and give them a reasonable deadline to reply (two to three weeks).

(4) Keep a copy of all correspondence. Never send original material without keeping a copy for yourself.

After the letter is written, send it by registered or certified mail (return receipt requested) so you have proof that you sent it. Allow a reasonable time for a response. If no response comes within a couple of weeks, write a follow-up letter and enclose a copy of your earlier letter. In most states, insurance companies are obliged to respond to your letters.

Failure to Acknowledge and Act Promptly on Communications with Respect to Claims Is an Unfair Insurance Claims Practice.

You may be surprised to learn that an insurance company will often pay your claim after hearing your side of the story. In many cases, the company will offer a compromise which could be a good solution if there is an honest dispute between you and the company. If the company persists in denying your claim, it may give you a further explanation which you may find satisfactory. On the other hand, such additional information may still not resolve the dispute to your satisfaction. You will then have two choices: you either forget your claim or keep persisting. If you believe that you are right, keep on pursuing matters.

Step 7: Seek Outside Help When Needed.

The following are suggestions for bringing extra pressure to bear on your insurance company, and are often successful measures for getting your claim paid satisfactorily. They need not be followed in the order presented. For example, you may want to go straight to a lawyer and bypass the State Department of Insurance, or vice versa. The important point is that you have exhausted all of your personal resources and efforts, and now it is time to bring out the heavy artillery. These stronger measures usually work. Also, these resources are usually free or at very little cost to you—yes, even a lawyer, if you get the right kind of lawyer.

A: YOUR STATE DEPARTMENT OF INSURANCE

If your effort at negotiating with a company has been unsuccessful, you may want to use the free services of your State Insurance Department. Departments of Insurance are state agencies headed by each state's insurance commissioner. The purpose of these agencies is to regulate fairness within the insurance industry and to help consumers with their insurance needs. Specifically, State Departments can function to help consumers find appropriate insurance coverage at affordable prices, assure rates are fair and reasonable, and prevent dishonest or deceptive marketing and sales practices. They also work to assure that claims are handled promptly and fairly. (For a list of all State Insurance Departments, see Appendix A.)

Although almost all State Departments of Insurance work to identify and prevent unfair claims practices, the degree to which they can help consumers with individual complaints often varies dramatically from state to state. Some states such as California, New York, and Illinois have strong, well-staffed insurance departments that can take an active interest in consumer disputes and will even act as a referee between you and your insurance company. However, many state governments lack the resources or inclination to become involved in individual complaints or are too influenced by the insurance lobby to set up an active consumer advocacy.

California is one state that conducts individual investigations. The California State Department of Insurance assures that every complaint is considered for all lines of insurance. If you are a resident of California and you think you have been treated unfairly by an insurance company, you can call the Department's toll-free hotline listed in Appendix A. The hotline unit is staffed with forty insurance experts who should be able to assist you directly and answer any questions you may have regarding your case. If you have an official complaint about the way your claim was handled, they will provide you with a complaint form to fill out and send back to them. They will then contact the insurance company and respond to you within 10 working days. When they respond, they will be able to tell you what action is being taken and the name of the expert handling your case. Your file will be kept open until you are satisfied and they can advise you how to proceed.

The California State Department also publishes two consumer studies: a complaint-ratio study and a rate-comparison study. The results of the complaint-ratio study tell you which companies have received the highest number of complaints in a given line of insurance, while the rate-comparison study gives you information on comparison shopping for any type of policy. This information is accessible by writing for it or through their toll-free hotline, as well. Also available are consumer guides on auto, homeowner's, worker's compensation, life, group and individual health, and other types of insurance. These guides can help you to become aware of your rights and to make informed insurance decisions. Some guides are now available in Spanish and Chinese.

B: Arbitration

Your next alternative to consider may be some form of arbitration, in which you and your insurance company split the cost of hiring an outside arbitrator. Arbitrators are impartial parties who listen to the facts of the dispute and make a decision that you and your insurance company must accept. You can locate one by calling an arbitration group such as Arbitration Forums (Phone: 800-426-8889) or the American Arbitration Association (Phone: 212-484-4000). Your right to arbitration is sometimes explicitly stated within the policy. Even if it is not, an insurance company is likely to agree to arbitration since the cost is considerably cheaper than that of a lawsuit. However, unless you are familiar with the rules of arbitration, this may not be a good choice because many arbitrations can get so technical and the procedures so detailed that the insurance company will enjoy an advantage over you. Also, check to see how much it will cost you and whether the decision of the arbitrator is binding or only advisory.

C: SMALL CLAIMS COURT

If your claim is less than the jurisdictional amount—the maximum amount for a claim that can be legally filed for in this court—of the small claims court in your state, you can take the company directly to court yourself without the assistance of a lawyer and frequently obtain quick results. The jurisdictional amount of small claims court is usually low, often in the neighborhood of $1,000 to $2,500. You can check your state's jurisdictional amount by calling the courthouse in your area. Remember, when you are listing your damages for your insurance company's failure to pay the claim, you may be entitled to mileage costs, incidental damages for postage, paperwork processing, telephone calls, and even your time for having to fight the battle.

If you are willing to go to small claims court and your claim is slightly more than the maximum limit of the court, to save time and expense, you may wish to reduce your claim to the jurisdictional limit. For example, if the small claims jurisdiction limit is $1,500 and your medical bills are

$1,600, you may file your small claims suit for $1,500 and forgive the extra $100. A small claims lawsuit will require that the company find someone to go to court for it, and this costs the company time and money. The very fact that you are willing to go to court may force the company to settle with you out of court.

D: A Lawyer

Finding and retaining a lawyer may not be as hard or costly as you think. Local bar associations and consumer-advocate groups may be able to refer you to a lawyer who is familiar with insurance company practices. If you don't want to lay out money for a lawyer, you can find one who will work for a *contingency fee*. This means that your lawyer collects his or her fee only if the case is won or a settlement is reached. By hiring a lawyer on a contingency basis, you will usually not have to put up any money to have your case prosecuted through the courts. If the lawyer doesn't win, you don't pay him. If the lawyer does win, the usual fee is one-third of the recovery, although this can vary depending on the complexity of the case. In some cases the lawyer may want to be reimbursed for expenses as the case goes along, but if you cannot afford this, most lawyers will put up the expenses for you and seek reimbursement out of the recovery. Since a contingency arrangement can be like a free ticket to the court system, which can bring you compensation over and above your claim, let's get into how it works:

**A Contingency Fee Permits the Policyholder
to Obtain Representation and Pay the Lawyer
a Specified Percentage of What the Lawyer
Eventually Recovers. If the Policyholder
Does Not Recover Any Damages, the
Policyholder Does Not Pay the Lawyer.**

There are many lawyers who are willing to take this type of case on a contingency basis. Generally, these lawyers are called trial lawyers. You can obtain information about trial lawyers in your state by writing to the Association of Trial Lawyers of America, 1050 31st Street, N.W., Washington, DC 20007 (Phone: 800-424-2725).

This organization publishes a directory of its members who take cases mostly on a contingency-fee basis and who generally represent people who have problems with insurance companies. In addition, most states have state trial lawyer organizations. These organizations will also be happy to provide information about their members. For a listing of the names and addresses of these organizations, see Appendix B.

Important items to consider when you are shopping for a lawyer are cost and quality—just like shopping for anything else. Do a little homework about your lawyer—check out his or her competence in the particular area of insurance involved in your claim, by asking people familiar with consumer-type lawyers, such as consumer organizations or even your insurance agent. *Always* make sure you understand the contingency-fee agreement *before* you sign a retainer. When you go to the lawyer's office for your initial interview, be sure you take your policy and any booklet or advertising material that relates to it, a copy of the claim form you submitted, all supporting documentation, and all of your correspondence with the company. Be prepared to discuss all aspects of your claim in order to enable the lawyer to evaluate your case thoroughly.

When an insurance company has denied a claim wrongfully, the policyholder and his or her family may experience emotional distress and other damages such as economic loss. In order to evaluate whether your case has merit, your lawyer will need adequate and truthful information on all aspects of your complaint. Be sure to tell the lawyer all of the hardships you have suffered because your claim was denied. Remember that lawyers have not been trained in psychiatry or medicine, and the scope of his or her abilities may cause the lawyer inadvertently to overlook some of the personal problems caused by the claim's denial. This is why your input is so important to determining the full, reasonable amount of your claim.

Even if you do not want to hire a lawyer immediately, it is often helpful to consult with one in order to determine your legal rights and to get his or her opinion as to the value of your claim. Generally, this first consultation will be free. A lawyer can usually help you to interpret your policy and to evaluate whether or not your claim was handled fairly. Many times, one phone call from a lawyer to an insurance company to let them know that you are being represented is all it takes for them to reconsider their position. The mere condition of being represented by a lawyer can have the effect of raising the value of your claim in the eyes of the insurance company—and may help impel them toward a more rapid settlement. This effect often results from an insurance company's respect for an attorney's superior negotiation skills, knowledge of all of the damages to which you are legally entitled, and ability to bring a case to trial, which can be costly to an insurance company.

E: THE "BAD FAITH" LAWSUIT

The most lethal weapon and the one most feared by insurance companies is a lawsuit charging them with handling your claim in "bad faith." To put it simply, in this context, "bad faith is the unreasonable refusal to promptly pay a valid claim." By law, your company has a legal duty to treat you in good faith because you have paid them money (your premiums) to protect you from financial loss. Bad faith can also encompass a company's failure to investigate a claim adequately, its unreasonable delay in claims processing, or its inadequate payment for the claim filed. Ordinarily, a policyholder is entitled only to the benefits set out in the policy, but:

If the Insurance Company Breached the Duty of Good Faith It Owes You as a Policyholder, You May Also Be Entitled to Recover Incidental Damages, Including Economic Loss and a Sum for Emotional Distress. If the Company Has Been Really Unscrupulous, the Law May Provide for Punitive Damages.

The law established the principle of punitive damages to serve as a deterrent to bad faith practices. Not all states have punitive-damages laws, but most states have some type of laws to protect policyholders from unfair claims practices and also allow other types of penalties or damages to be imposed.

The case studies that follow are a cross-section of cases in which individuals took their complaints all the way through jury trials—and won. If you take your case all the way, the chances are that a jury of your peers will decide correctly which side is right. If your side is right, the jury will decide on the amount you should receive. Don't be afraid to let a jury resolve your dispute. It is the fairest and most democratic institution in our society.

Insurance companies want to do away with everything from punitive damages to the jury trial itself. If you doubt this, look at some of the advertisements the insurance companies are placing in our national magazines. Although it has become quite popular to denounce our litigious society and to condemn lawyers and claimants seeking relief in courts as overzealous and even greedy, the civil suit seeking punitive damages for wrongful conduct is the most effective weapon available to citizens challenging abuses by insurance companies and other corporations. Never has the need to bring these corporate malefactors to account been more urgent.

CHAPTER 4

How the Legal System Can Work for You

The case studies found in the next chapters are actual court cases of typical American consumers who possessed the courage and tenacity to seek justice against insurance company abuse by taking the companies in question to court.

I've practiced insurance law on behalf of the consumer since the early 1970's. When I began trying these cases, there were hardly any trial lawyers around who had even heard of this emerging new facet of law now called "bad faith." Today, trial lawyers across the country are pursuing bad faith insurance cases on behalf of policyholders.

My first taste of victory in a bad faith insurance case occurred in 1971—just about the time when this legal concept was in its embryonic stages in California. I represented Otis Drake, age 59, a farmer who suffered from severe emphysema. For years he had spread manure over acres of farmland in the valley near Chino, California. Finally, his emphysema became so disabling that he had extreme difficulty breathing and could barely walk.

Otis had a disability policy with Pennsylvania Life and was receiving disability income, when suddenly, after a few months, the company cut off his benefits. The carrier said that, if Drake could walk even a few blocks, he was not house-confined and was therefore ineligible for disability benefits under the policy terms. Otis's first lawyer made little progress with the insurance carrier. Then, because he worked on an hourly rate—a fee he knew Otis could not afford—he referred Drake to me because he knew I took cases on a contingency-fee basis. I carefully revieweu the case. Having grown up in a farming community, I had empathy for the hardworking farmer, so I was outraged at the attitude of the insurance company. I agreed to represent Otis on a contingency basis.

Otis Drake was one of the most honest and pleasant individuals I had ever met. I was hoping the jury would fall in love with him and his wonderful wife. But—most important—I knew that Penn Life's decision was absolutely wrong. After a long trial in San Bernardino County Superior Court, the jury awarded Otis all of his disability benefits, plus $325,000 in punitive damages.

After the Drake victory, I began to realize that insurance abuse was widespread. Regulatory efforts by state insurance commissioners were minimal. As I reviewed one victim's story after another, I soon realized that as long as insurance has been part of the American way of life, policyholders have faced difficulty in challenging the decisions of their insurance carriers.

Battles with insurance companies are as old as insurance itself. Consider the story of William Gybbons, a life-insurance policyholder in sixteenth-century England. Gybbons had signed a yearlong contract with an insurance carrier to protect his wife as he was going on a long sea journey. After he returned, he died unexpectedly, shortly before the calendar year ended. However, the insurer asserted, "twelve lunar months of twenty-eight days apiece" had expired, and, therefore, denied Gybbons's wife the benefits. The family took the case to court and eventually won. Yet, in the ensuing 400 years, the insurance industry has developed thousands of ways to deny legitimate claims. No wonder the average American has little affection for his or her insurance company.

Insurance is supposed to spread the risk. But, from cases I have investigated, insurance carriers are spreading something other than risk. While the insurance industry continues to amass a huge share of the corporate wealth in America, the average legitimate claimant must rely on his insurer's benevolence for the protection he or she assumed was promised by a policy.

Many insurance claims are handled routinely without much trouble. Yet the lack of any meaningful regulation has created a growing climate of abuse toward policyholders. Insurance companies insist they sell protection. But, as soon as a policyholder files a claim, an adversarial attitude sets in. The attitude suggests that a policyholder is automatically wrong and the insurance company is automatically right. Building on this assumption, the carrier can use endless technicalities, exclusions, and ambiguities to say "claim denied." The insurance adjuster always seems to enter the revolving door behind you and come out ahead of you.

Many policyholders settle a claim for less than is due them, accepting such diminished reimbursement as an unpleasant— but incontestable—fact of life. Rather than being rescued by the heroic images used by insurance companies, such as Paul Revere, John Hancock, or Thomas Jefferson, policyholders become victimized by accusations. In extreme instances, they are charged with dishonesty, arson, malingering, or fraud. Understandably, policyholders quickly perceive their insurers as enemies. Indeed, one may have lost one's health, house, car, and even family members—and now faces the loss of self-respect while defending oneself against the charges of one's insurance company. Sad to say, such bitter clashes between insured and insurer are by no means isolated instances. You need only look at the insurance cases pending in courts nationwide to realize just how widespread the problem has become. And as the stakes rise—with staggering increases in medical costs a prime factor—you are likely to find insurance companies scrambling even harder to find the loophole that allows them to deny, or effectively discourage, claims which you— the policyholder—have solid reasons to consider reasonable and payable.

Isn't it ironic that when we hear about insurance cheats, the first image that comes to mind is that of the guy who falsified a claim in order to reap a bonanza from his insurance company? The industry public-relations mills have created a phantom American policyholder who stages an auto accident, burns down his house, injures himself to avoid work, and, in extreme cases, even kills off relatives to collect death benefits.

Of course, we are not about to deny that consumer fraud exists. When it occurs, all consumers suffer—in the pocketbook and in the unnecessary distrust created in the system. A carrier should not have to pay false claims. Insurance agents need time to investigate a claim thoroughly in order to make a sound and fair decision. But to what extent is consumer fraud—as opposed to insurance fraud—occurring? Are both treated with equal weight under the law?

If a policyholder inflates property or auto damages, sets his car on fire, or commits arson, he is breaking the law and should be punished. Indeed, in cases such as these, a district attorney will often enter the case and the consumer can end up in jail. But how many insurance adjusters do you know who have been indicted for fraud? White-collar insurance executives—caught in well-documented corporate crime against policyholders—do not end up in jail.

Meanwhile, the honest policyholders—who represent the large majority of consumers—feel ever more isolated and vulnerable when confronted with problems collecting legitimate benefits. Who is taking up their cause? Thousands of policyholders write letters of complaint to insurance companies, which go largely unanswered. Any response is usually doubletalk, peppered with meaningless standard insurance jargon.

Until about 15 years ago, the notion of real discipline and punishment for insurance fraud against policyholders was a joke. Then the California courts provided policyholders and those who represented them with a powerful legal weapon, and the concept of insurance "bad faith" was born. Currently, a majority of states have followed California's lead and have adopted some form of "bad faith" law.

The law of bad faith is simple. If a policyholder's claim has been unreasonably denied, he or she can sue for more than the amount of his or her benefits. The insured can collect damages for mental suffering and all economic loss caused by the company's refusal to honor a legitimate claim. If it can be shown that the insurance company's conduct demonstrated a conscious disregard for the rights of a policyholder, then the policyholder can sue and recover punitive damages. The purpose of punitive damages is to punish and make examples of companies that engage in outrageous behavior. A jury sets the amount of punitive damages based on the amount of money it will take to make an errant company change operating procedures and behave more responsibly.

The true stories that follow are about honorable people who would not accept denial of benefits by their insurance companies. Put bluntly, they told their insurance companies to go to hell, dragged them into court, and asked that they be punished. They took the crucial step that government agencies, by and large, have failed to take on behalf of consumers.

In my law practice, I hear insurance horror stories every day. I hear of families hounded by collection agencies to pay medical bills that insurance companies should have paid. I hear of disabled people who are forced to go on welfare instead of collecting disability benefits due them under an insurance policy. In one case, a rental company actually repossessed a policyholder's wheelchair because the insurance carrier failed to make payments. One woman became so distraught because the company would not pay her medical bills that she attempted suicide. Some businesses, large and small, have gone bankrupt when reluctant insurance companies refused to make timely payments on legitimate claims.

The punishment handed out by juries against insurance companies in individual cases has been beneficial to all consumers. Jury verdicts are helping to diminish the power gap between the large insurance company, with its unlimited funds and a heavily staffed legal department, and the small consumer. Thanks to bad faith lawsuits, the insurance industry no longer enjoys the freedom to practice what it pleases on whom it pleases.

The law's message is clear: today, those who abuse the free marketplace can be brought to justice and punished severely—not by the government, but by the no-longer-passive policyholder, the consumer, who is determined that he or she will not be victimized any longer.

It is my hope that the cases presented here will serve a twofold purpose. I hope they will encourage all readers who feel they have had a claim unjustly denied—or who suffered some other form of insurance company abuse—to fight back, to go the extra mile to get the benefits that are rightfully due them.

I also trust that, in reading through these cases, readers

will discover additional facts and tips that—taken together with the information already provided—will help them work effectively as individuals, with intermediaries, or with lawyers, to successfully pursue a legitimate claim until they have achieved full satisfaction.

CHAPTER 5

You Can Fight Back and Win

Case Study: *Egan v. Mutual of Omaha*

Some years ago, Michael Egan, a muscular 55-year-old roofer, fell off a ladder. He had begun his day like thousands before, constructing rooftops in Pomona, California. But this morning, as he stepped down the ladder, a rung broke. Mike plunged 12 feet to the ground, injuring his back severely.

Mike had carried a Mutual of Omaha disability insurance policy for years. The policy promised to pay $200 a month for life if Mike became totally disabled by an accident. Following his mishap, Mutual of Omaha paid benefits, but cut them off abruptly several months later. By the time a year had passed, Mike had no other choice but to sue.

The trial reflected a classic confrontation. Mike, a stout Irish immigrant with a grade-school education, worked most of his life as a roofer. He had a disabled wife and a young daughter.

On the other side of the courtroom sat attorneys for Mutual of Omaha—self-acclaimed as the largest accident and health insurance company in the world.

Mike's case was simple. He hurt his back falling off a roof.

After about six months of conservative therapy, the injury required back surgery. Unfortunately, the operation was unsuccessful, and the doctors declared Mike totally disabled.

Classification of Mike's injury as a sickness or an accident became the pivotal point in the case because accident payments were for life, and sickness payments stopped in three months. Mutual of Omaha opened Mike's file as an accident claim, but, for mysterious reasons, converted the accident claim to a sickness claim. The decision to reclassify the claim occurred at about the same time that Mike's total disability became obvious. The switch meant that he would be eligible for only three more months of benefits. Mike had no choice but to head straight for the courtroom.

I opened the trial with Michael Egan, his wife, Mary, and daughter, Maureen, telling their stories. They were believable and sympathetic witnesses. They told how Mutual's Los Angeles claims manager, Andrew McEachen, came to the Egan home and said that Mutual had decided to cut Mike's payments off. He charged that Mike could work if he wanted to—that he was merely malingering.

Upset, Mike denied the manager's accusations. He told the manager that his disability had left him distraught about money. The family testified that McEachen laughed at Mike during the visit and called him a fraud. Mike, normally a strong man, began to cry. His wife and daughter were distraught. Mike was angry and humiliated.

There was a second personal visit to Mike's home, this time from Mutual claims adjuster Michael Segal. He argued that Mike's disability had been caused by sickness, and therefore he was no longer eligible for disability. Segal then told Mike that, if he would surrender his policy, Mutual would give him a generous payment.

After Segal's visit, Mike confirmed his diagnosis with his surgeon, Dr. Donald Carpenter, who again classified Mike as totally disabled. Mike wrote Segal in Los Angeles and requested continued payment of his disability benefits. Mike kept a copy of the letter but never received a response.

Because his injury had occurred on the job, Mike had also filed a worker's compensation claim; he received a high disability rating. Having exhausted their personal savings, the Egan family lived on worker's compensation.

Mike never returned to work and continued seeking regular medical care. Doctors referred him to a rehabilitation program; but after exhaustive tests, they told him that rehabilitation efforts were impossible. Under extreme financial stress, the Egans eventually had to borrow money in order to live. This family, dependent upon the good faith of Mutual of Omaha, was left in financial shambles and emotional chaos.

I called Mike's attending doctor, Dr. Stephen Odgers, to the stand. Dr. Odgers explained Mike's severe medical condition, his surgery, and how Mike's condition resulted from his fall.

Next, the jury needed to hear from Mutual of Omaha. I called Segal as an adverse witness. First, I wanted to make it clear that Mike was totally disabled.

Shernoff: "There was no question that Mr. Egan was totally disabled as far as the policy goes?"

Segal: "Right. I don't believe the question of total disability ever was raised."

Q. "It was just accident versus sickness?"

A. "Yes."

Next, I had to destroy Mutual of Omaha's possible argument that some sort of sickness, such as arthritis, caused Mike's disability. I proceeded directly to establish that it was not caused by a sickness.

Throughout the trial, Segal had argued that the home office had decided to deny Mike's claim. I was sure that Segal would try to blame someone in the home office. This was indeed the case. However, in a report back to the home office, Segal had concluded with the phrase "best to handle on the basis of sickness." I seized upon that statement. I intended to demonstrate that the classification conversion from "accident" to "sickness" devastated Mike and profited Mutual of Omaha by a tidy sum.

Shernoff: "Now, you have this phrase here, down three lines from the bottom, 'Best to handle on the basis of sickness.' "

Segal: "Yes."

Q. "Now, at that time you wrote that you, of course, knew that if you handled it on the basis of sickness you would be depriving Mr. Egan of some 20 years of benefits and that he would only receive three months' benefits; is that correct?"

A. "Well, I base claims on—on facts, not—when I base—but, I mean, I handle claims on the information."

Q. "Excuse me . . . the question was, at the time you wrote that—"

A. "Yes."

Q. "—you knew you had knowledge of the fact that if you handled it as sickness he would be cut off after three months?"

A. "Yes."

Q. "Okay. Now, when you said, 'Best to handle on the basis of sickness,' what did you mean by that? Was this best for Mr. Egan?"

A. "No."

Q. "Now, this decision to close on the basis of sickness is really quite an important decision from the company's standpoint, is it not?"

A. "Yes."

Q. "As a matter of fact, we can figure it out mathematically. It amounts to about a $40,000 decision, doesn't it?"

A. "As I look at it now, yes, sir."

Q. "And the $40,000 decision, certainly with your experience with the company, is quite carefully reviewed by people in high authority, is it not?"

A. "Well, I would say generally most files are reviewed."

Having pried these admissions out of Segal, I proceeded to pound away on how little investigation Segal had carried out to determine whether Mike's disability originated from a sickness or an accident. I wanted to show that Mutual of Omaha did not want a thorough investigation; with hardly any evidence, they had rushed through a reclassification with the sole purpose of saving money. Segal went a long way toward proving my point.

Shernoff: "Well . . . in all fairness, you are cutting this man's benefits off on the basis of some sickness in his back just shortly after you know he has surgery. Did you at least check, let's say, with his doctor who had been treating him for eight or nine years to see whether or not his doctor would agree that some disease was going on?"

Segal: "No, that wasn't done."

Q. "Did you check with the doctor who did the surgery on his back whether in his opinion the surgery was necessitated by the fall or whether the surgery was due to some sort of rare disease?"

A. "Well, I didn't check myself, no, sir."

Q. "Wouldn't that have been the proper thing to do, sir?"

A. "I believe so."

Q. "Having looked at the file and having sat here the best part of the day and answered questions, do you have any opinion as to whether or not this claim was handled properly [at the time]?"

A. "Well, I have pondered this considerably, and I feel there could have been some more handling done at that time."

Segal's testimony placed Mutual of Omaha in a real bind. The jury had already seen how the Egan family had suffered considerably at the company's hands. Now here was Segal virtually admitting that reclassifying Mike's claim from accident to sickness had little justification—except to save the company $40,000. Segal admitted that there was little investigation, but he insisted that others directed him to do it. Who was responsible? The jury wanted to know.

I next called Segal's boss, McEachan—who didn't help Mutual of Omaha either. He said he did not harass Mike in his home, but the jury did not believe him. When I shot a direct question at him about whether the termination of Egan's benefits was right or wrong, McEachan became flustered.

Shernoff: "You know Mr. Egan's benefits, what might have been lifetime benefits, were terminated on the basis of sickness, do you not?"

McEachan: "Yes, I do."

Q. "Do you feel that the action by the company was wrong?"

A. "I feel that you have this—"

He paused a long time. I started to get restless. The judge was waiting, too.

Shernoff: "Can he answer yes or no, Your Honor?"

The Court: "I think you can answer the question, please, Mr. McEachan."

McEachan: "There could be a question, yes. I meant, could be more information that may be necessary in order to—but this is hindsight, I mean. Truly I mean maybe I am kind of dense."

I felt a sense of relief after this testimony. McEachan obviously attempted to perform his best to justify Mutual of Omaha's conduct, but the truth became so obvious that he simply fell apart.

Another claims analyst, Frank Romano, was also persuaded to admit that Mutual's investigation was pathetic, at best.

Shernoff: "Can you tell us why Dr. Carpenter wasn't consulted about this?"

Romano: "No, sir, I can't tell you why he wasn't consulted."

Q. "Can you tell us why Dr. Odgers wasn't consulted?"

A. "No, sir, I can't."

Q. "Can you tell us why action was taken to terminate Mr. Egan's benefits without consulting one medical doctor?"

A. "No, sir, I can't."

Q. "That's quite improper, isn't it?"

A. "It would be wrong, I believe, yes."

Now all three adjusters admitted that the insurance carrier's actions were wrong. Mutual of Omaha's attorneys realized the obvious; their strategy now was to turn against the local adjusters, Segal and McEachan, and try to cut them loose. The home office knew nothing of this travesty, argued the attorneys. If the strategy worked, the jury might sympathize with an honest company that simply had two rotten eggs.

The trial's focus shifted. The question became: who was responsible for the dirty work—the local adjusters or the home office?

Mutual of Omaha called Willard Gustin, the home office manager of the Continuing Disability Benefits Department. Gustin took the stand and explained that the authority to terminate claims such as Egan's rested with local adjusters. The home office file on Egan, he said, had been misplaced mysteriously. It was just lost somewhere, "as can happen in large corporations," for a period of time. The file must have fallen in a "corporate crack" for a while, he said. This "corporate crack" threatened to swallow Mutual when I confronted Gustin in cross-examination and made his story fall apart piece by piece.

First, I showed that Mike had written a letter to the home office complaining about the reclassification. That letter was not in the home office file, and its absence was suspicious. Then I tried to show that even if the file had fallen in a crack—back at the home office—they certainly should have discovered it in response to an inquiry from the Department of Insurance some nine months before the lawsuit was filed. This line of questioning took Gustin somewhat by surprise.

Shernoff: "Sir, even if it fell into that crack, if someone would specifically call your attention to it, then there would be an analysis. Right?"

Gustin: "Absolutely."

Q. "So, sir, isn't it true that in this case Mutual of Omaha's attention was called to this very situation at least one year before this lawsuit was filed by the Department of Insurance, State of California, and to this day your company hasn't responded to that request?"

He didn't reply.

I subsequently showed him the letter from the Department of Insurance.

Shernoff: "Sir, isn't it true . . . that approximately nine months before this lawsuit was filed, the Department of Insurance called the attention of Mutual of Omaha to a complaint filed in this case with reference to Mr. Egan? Didn't they ask you to actually look into it, analyze it, and report back to them within 15 days?"

A. "Yes, sir."

Q. "Okay. Let me just ask you this question, sir. Do you know whether a report was sent back, if an analysis was done and sent back to the Department of Insurance as requested either within 15 days or to this very day?"

A. "I don't know anything about it."

Q. "Certainly should have been done, should it not, sir?"

A. "I can only answer this way, that upon the receipt of the letter it should have gone to one of the staff in the department that handles this sort of thing."

Q. "Certainly as of that date, even if the file fell in that deep, wide crack, someone would be obliged to pick it up and analyze it and see what happened; is that right?"

A. "It would appear so."

The "corporate crack" theory began to fizzle. How could Mike's file be misplaced at the home office? First Mike had written a letter complaining, and then the State Department of Insurance had made an inquiry. Furthermore, I had written a letter offering to settle the case without a lawsuit if the company would restore Mike's disability benefits and pay attorneys' fees. Surely these events would have alerted home office personnel to seek out such a crucial file, wherever it had been mislaid. Yet Gustin stuck to his theory: the local level did the dirty work, and the home office didn't know what was going on.

This line of defense fell apart when Mutual's lawyer questioned Gustin, and he referred innocently to a "file jacket." I had the entire claims file in my possession and I had neither heard of nor seen a file jacket! I pounced upon this file jacket testimony.

Shernoff: "Now, sir, with reference to that particular file, I notice that you alluded to the fact that there was a jacket usually on those claims files; is that correct?"

Gustin: "A green jacket that is a facing type of thing, yes." [It should be noted that this jacket was to be initialed by anyone borrowing the file for review.]

Q. "So, if we had the notations on the jacket, we would know who saw the file at what times?"

A. "Well, yes and no. . . . I don't think you can dogmatically make a statement, you know, that this is a hundred percent."

We were not getting very far with this questioning. I wanted the file jacket.

Q. "Do you know where the jacket of that file is?"

A. "Well, it should be—I don't know where it is, if this is what you are asking me, no."

Q. "This was represented to us as a full and complete file."

I showed the court my copy, that it did not have the critical file jacket. The jury knew there was a file jacket that might expose who saw the file in the home office, when, and perhaps for what purpose. Mysteriously absent from Mutual's original documents, the file jacket was in Omaha. The court ordered the company to produce it immediately, and it arrived by air courier the next day.

When I first read the file jacket, I knew I had hit pay dirt. During its entire trial, Mutual of Omaha had asserted that its home office had not seen this file during the crucial period around the preceding May, when the company had reclassified Mike's claim from accident to sickness.

Now, we had a file jacket with approximately 20 dated stamps during that crucial period. At least 20 times during those critical six months, various people had looked at the file and initialed it.

When the trial resumed, I cautiously approached Gustin. I held up the file jacket; and, as the jurors looked on, I asked:

Shernoff: "We can safely say, then, even before this lawsuit was filed in February, that the people back at Mutual of Omaha looked at their file or wanted to look at their file and actually did look at their file, according to the jacket, probably at least 20 times; is that correct?"

Gustin: "For one reason or another."

It now appeared Mutual of Omaha had sunk into its own "corporate crack." I was sure that the jury by now believed that the company hadn't treated Michael Egan very fairly in the first place. Now Mutual's attempt to shove all the blame onto its lower-echelon adjusters was exposed.

I knew then the case was going beautifully.

My last task was to produce evidence of Mutual of Omaha's financial worth and to sum up. In a punitive damage case, a jury can hear evidence of the company's worth in order to set the appropriate punishment.

Every State Insurance Department requires insurance companies conducting business in that state to file a complete yearly financial report. It is a public record and provides detailed financial information about the company, including all assets, liabilities, net worth, and income for the preceding year. In order to show the jury Mutual of Omaha's financial condition, I had subpoenaed those annual reports. I wanted the jury to receive a complete and up-to-date financial picture of Mutual of Omaha's assets.

Mutual's lawyers were not content to let these statements speak for themselves. Economic conditions at that time were not the best for insurance companies, and it was true that Mutual of Omaha's income was down a bit, as was most insurance income. The company introduced Mutual of Omaha's comptroller, Marvin Maher, in a futile attempt to convince the jury that Mutual of Omaha faced hard times. After all, Mutual of Omaha wasn't that big, they argued.

But Maher's testimony opened the door for me to reveal another of Mutual's attempts to pull the wool over the jurors' eyes. I began cross-examination with the most recent annual report on file with the California Department of Insurance.

Shernoff: "Okay. Now, sir, let's get to the assets of this company as we are talking about the California statement now. Give us the total assets of this small company, sir."

Maher: "The total assets are $756,596,000. I have rounded that off."

Q. "As I understand it, of that $756,000,000, you have got how much in bonds that you have invested in?"

A. "$556,335,745.24."

Q. "And how much in preferred stocks?"

A. "In preferred stocks, $23,982,503.23."

Q. "And how much in common stocks?"

A. "In common stocks, $152,180,159.48."

Q. "How about just plain old cash on hand?"

A. "Cash, $15,953,954.58."

Q. "Now, sir, can you tell us the net gain from operations before dividends to policyholders and before federal income taxes and excluding capital gains and losses for the year?"

A. "It was $27,153,394.92."

Q. "So, as I understand that figure, that 27 million dollars, that is what the net profit or net gain of the company was before you take off dividends to policyholders and income taxes; is that correct?"

A. "That is right, sir."

Q. "You did pay a dividend to life policyholders that has to be subtracted from that. Is that correct?"

A. "Yes, that was $254,653.98."

Q. "And dividends on accident and health policies. How much did you pay on that?"

A. "We paid zero on that."

Q. "Right. Perhaps you can answer this question for me. And before we get to the taxes, it appears that you made some $27,000,000. Could you explain to us why no dividends were paid to people who owned the accident and health policies?"

A. "Well, it is just our policy not to pay a cash dividend to them."

Q. "So your net gain is how much?"

A. "$26,898,740.94."

Q. "And—out of this $26,000,000 profit—$26,898,000—how much did you pay in federal income taxes that year?"

A. "The amount incurred was $2,391,776.01."

Q. "So, after the income taxes and after the dividends and after everything . . . you still had how much left over in profit?"

A. "$24,506,964.03."

The jury got the picture. Mutual of Omaha was not a small and vulnerable company. Rather, the finances reflected exactly what Mutual of Omaha advertised—the company was one of the largest accident and health insurance companies in the world.

Dividends and taxes were significant figures, too. Taxes were 10 percent. Most people on the jury paid substantially more than 10 percent in federal income taxes, and I knew they would wonder why a company that made $26 million per year paid only approximately 10 percent in taxes. It was also startling that Mutual of Omaha paid no cash dividends to its accident and health policyholders. After all, a mutual company is owned by the policyholders—at least in theory—and they should be getting a yearly dividend out of the profits. Although the life policyholders received a cash dividend, the accident and health policyholders—representing 90 percent of the business—did not. I delved into these points with Maher. I wanted to show the jury where all the money was really going and how much Mutual of Omaha had amassed in its surplus account over the years. (The surplus account in insurance company accounting is the rough equivalent to the net worth of the company.)

Maher reviewed two or three additional financial statements, and even though there were fluctuations year to year, I persuaded Maher to admit that whenever the Dow-Jones stock index goes up a few points, Mutual makes a few million. Perhaps the most devastating part of Maher's cross-examination surfaced as I concentrated on Mutual of Omaha's failure to pay cash dividends to the accident and health policyholders. The financial statement for the year showed that the surplus account was up to about $200 million.

Shernoff: "Now, this surplus account, you don't, as I understand it, give any of this surplus back to these accident and health policyholders by way of distribution or dividends, do you?"

Maher: "Yes, sir, we do."

Q. "You indicated yesterday you only give them a rider."

A. "I indicated yesterday we do not return money to them in the form of a dividend per se as a person knows or is familiar with. That, you pay out of dividend in cash. We do offer a travel accident death rider as a part of the additional coverage on their policy, and this is, as I said yesterday, given to the policy owners at no increase in their premium."

Q. "You can't spend that, can you sir?"

A. "Yes, sir."

Q. "Can you go in a grocery store and buy groceries with that?"

A. "Yes, sir, the beneficiary can."

Q. "If he has an accident."

A. "If the beneficiary's spouse has an accident."

Q. "Right, but if you don't have an accidental death, you can't spend it?"

A. "Right. That is true."

Q. "And, as a matter of fact, as far as dividends or distributions to the policyholders in what we con-

sider the normal sense of someone getting a dividend, getting money back, getting a check and, as
you have so stated in your reports, there is no
distribution or dividend of this surplus money,
cash to the policyholders?"

A. "That is correct."

Q. "And the policyholders as you have indicated own
about 90 percent of the company? In other words,
they represent some 90 percent of the income?"

A. "The policy owners own our entire company. And
every cent that we show as surplus belongs to our
policy owners."

Q. "They don't get a nickel of it, of the cash?

After some additional questioning, I continued:

Q. "Now, sir, the policyholders of this company, the
so-called owners, as we have already indicated,
get no cash distribution, all they really get, sir—
all they really have is a hope and a promise if they
get injured or sick that the company will pay them
in accordance with the policy; is that right?"

A. "Well, sir, I would like not to refer to them as the so-
called policy owners. In a mutual company we rec-
ognize them as the policyholders. To answer your
question: Yes. This is why they took out the insurance, as protection. Now, I would like to add—"

Q. "Like Mr. Egan did?"

A. "Sir?" [Maher seemed a little surprised.]

Q. "Like Mr. Egan did? He is an owner, isn't he?"

A. "Yes, sir."

My voice was filled with indignation as I finished. The
jury heard what had happened to Michael Egan. Now they
knew the company made a handsome profit, possessed a

surplus account of about $200 million at the end of the year, and paid no cash dividends to accident and health policyholders. The company's feeble attempt to explain the substituted dividend of a small travel accident death policy did not go very far. This type of policy, I quickly pointed out, cost Mutual of Omaha very little in actual dollars.

So, where did the money go? It certainly wasn't distributed back to the policyholders. And from what the jury heard, policyholders like Mike did not receive a fair shake on claims either. The government received little from Mutual of Omaha in the form of taxes. Nor did the company's employees receive much of the income. Indeed, as a result of cross-examination, it seemed that most of the company's fortune either went to its high executives in salaries and benefits, or was stockpiled in Mutual's surplus account.

Closing arguments are very important because they give the lawyers the opportunity not only to review the factual evidence, but also to suggest ways to punish the company. I knew that the judge's instruction to the jury on punitive damages would tell them to consider not only Mutual of Omaha's financial worth, but the responsibility of the company's conduct. He would also say that punitive damages should bear a reasonable relationship to actual damages. The heart of my argument ran as follows:

> "The case really transcends Michael Egan. He is involved in it, but it is not only for Michael Egan and, as you will see, the case has implications far and wide. You 12 people sitting there are going to decide this case. . . . And your job will be to apply the facts to the law and render a just and fair verdict as you see it.
>
> "Now, in this case we have an obvious situation. A hardworking man, who really never took a dime from anybody in his life. All his life really involves, like most people, is working hard for his family,

doing what he is trained and experienced to do. He asks nothing of anybody that he doesn't deserve.

"One day he falls off a ladder. It puts him out of commission for the rest of his life, basically. . . . An obvious accident, obvious to anybody. I mean, you don't have to have medical training to know that [falling off a ladder] is an accident.

"Here we have a company, a large company, probably—well, those figures we heard about—I don't know what sums you people are used to dealing with, but those figures to me are something that you read about, hear about.

"What do they do to Michael Egan?

"When it becomes obvious that this is a claim that may be a lifetime benefit, that may expose the company to $40,000 worth of benefits, that's the time that all of a sudden a classification conversion is made to sickness.

"They go to his house and call him a phony and a fraud and harass him right in his home in front of his wife and his child. It leaves them all crying. The company set up a nonexistent dispute that perhaps, maybe, they can get him to surrender his policy. . . . That's not decent, it's not right, it's reprehensible."

It was obvious that I was angry and that I perceived Mutual's treatment of Mike to be outrageous, but I wanted to make sure that this business-minded jury would not get the idea that I was antibusiness. I had to put this case in its proper context.

"Let me stop right here, because I think some people may be saying, Bill Shernoff, you really must be antibusiness. Well, that is not true. There are a lot of good businesses around, and there are a lot of good insurance companies around. A lot of them are making money honestly. Every honest, decent insurance company wants the unscrupulous ones to be punished. And I am not even saying there aren't good and decent people in this company. I am sure there are. But the point is there is a cancer there somewhere. You are the surgeons, and I am going to ask you to cure it."

After commenting on the evidence and asking the jury to compensate Mike Egan by awarding him his disability benefits and a fair amount for mental and emotional distress, I turned to the critical area of punitive damages. I first discussed the law of punitive damages with the jury.

"Now, we get to the second kind of damages, which are known as punitive damages. Now, we leave Mike Egan for a minute. I want to spend the remainder of my time talking about punitive damages. I feel this is absolutely the most important aspect of this case. There are going to be several jury instructions on punitive damages. I am going to leave the instructions to the Court, because you will hear what the law is on punitive damages. It is fair to say that it boils down to the proposition that for the sake of an example you can assess punitive damages if you find that the company acted either with malice, and that term will be defined for you by the Judge, or— and I say 'or' and not 'and'—or fraud, and that term will be defined for you by the Judge. The malice and fraud definitions embody a paragraph. Oppression is just one sentence: [reads] 'Oppression' means subjecting a person to cruel and unjust hardship in conscious disregard of his rights.

"Well, you don't even have to look for fraud or malice in this case, although I think both of them are there in abundance. But certainly Mike Egan was subjected to cruel and unjust hardship in conscious disregard of his rights."

I was now obliged to talk about punishment. I had to drive home the fact that the punitive award was not to compensate Mike Egan, but to punish Mutual of Omaha. I knew I would have to give the jury some logical guidelines. I had to correlate the concept of punishment with an appropriate amount of money.

"When we talk about punishing this corporation, we may be talking about an awful lot of money. Money is relative. Say we are talking about $2,000,000; that is a lot of money. It is not a lot of money if you want to buy a 747—it wouldn't even get you a tail. So it is relative. What's a lot of money? The Judge will tell you, in determining the amount necessary to impose the appropriate punitive effect, if you feel punitive damages should be awarded, you are entitled to consider the wealth and assets of the company.

"Let me give you a few examples. Let's take Mr. Segal; his assets or net worth, he says, are about $10,000 or $20,000. Let's take $10,000. If you punish Mr. Segal $10,000, that wouldn't be punishment, it would be persecution. You're not going to take away the guy's bank account; I don't think that is fair to anybody. However, maybe a $1,000 punishment or at least a $500 might be appropriate: a $1,000, for example, if you assume he has got $10,000 net worth—I am not talking about assets—I am talking about assets and subtracting liabilities . . . $1,000 is ten percent of his net worth.

"If you apply the same standard to Mutual of Omaha and take their surplus, whichever figure you want to take—there have been three of them mentioned here, $200,000,000. $162,000,000, and I think there was one in between, $194,000,000; and 10 percent of the lowest one is $16,000,000. That sounds like a lot of money, but you are applying the exact same standard to them as you are to Mr. Segal. What's just for the poor is just for the rich. Everybody is supposed to be guided and judged by the same standards of justice in this country.

"Another way to logically support [your verdict] is on the basis of earnings. We punish people on the basis of earnings all the time. You will see in the financial report that last year they made something like $26,000,000 after taxes, and boy, the taxes, 10 percent taxes. I would like to pay only 10 percent taxes. And if you look real thoroughly, in that annual report, you will find out how much property tax they paid on the building down on Wilshire Boulevard; it was zero. I would say in a case of this sort maybe a month or two of earnings would be appropriate. If you are making eight or nine hundred dollars a month and you get caught stealing, or whatever— swindle, fraud, malice, oppression—we might say a fair punishment would be a couple of months' earnings.

I concluded my summary to the jury with these remarks:

"Their own pledge is to support right principles and oppose bad practices in health and accident insurance. There is nothing in this country at this moment, and I think everybody knows that, that will do more to support right principles and oppose bad practices in health and accident insurance [than a large punitive damage verdict]. There is nothing that the legislature can do or will do that is [more meaningful] than what you people do here in this courtroom. And if it is not meaningful enough, it just is going to be something that they get away with again."

Both of Mutual of Omaha's lawyers were allowed to make closing arguments to the jury. One of them, Mr. Wild, tried to convince the jury that Mutual of Omaha made some mistakes but there was no intent to defraud Mike Egan. Mr. Doutre, Mutual's other attorney, got up and really took after me as just another plaintiff's attorney making phony arguments and looking for a pot of gold. Doutre approached the jury box and tried to divert their attention from all the damaging evidence against Mutual of Omaha by attacking me. He finally ended with:

"But I tell you that this argument—these arguments you have been getting concerning this punishment and these punitive damages against Mutual of Omaha are essentially false, phony arguments. They just—you know, let's get the pot of gold, 'Let's get the big score,' and that's about it."

Fortunately, the plaintiff gets the last word in closing arguments. The court always allows the plaintiff's lawyer a short rebuttal. We had put on a straightforward and sincere case, and I thought it was a big mistake for Mutual's lawyers to attack me. I spoke for only five minutes, reminding the jury what this case was all about. This wasn't a personality contest, this was important business. I never was more sincere in my life than when I told the jury my last words.

"Nobody is trying to break any company. I certainly wouldn't even suggest that in the least. But we do have a lot of people around that believe very strongly in decent and honest practices in the business, and they are all rooting for you. There are a lot of people that will be sick and disabled in this country in the future and shouldn't be cheated out of their money; they're all rooting for you. And, believe me, ladies and gentlemen, every one of those people [is] counting on you and your good judgment and your sense of basic fairness and decency. And I just pray that someone gives you the power to see what is right and do what is right."

The jury deliberated for about two days. They awarded Michael Egan $45,600 in past and future benefits under his disability policy, $78,000 for mental and emotional distress, and a record-setting $5.1 million in punitive damages.

The verdict streaked through the insurance community and the press. Headlines appeared in dailies nationwide, from the *Los Angeles Times,* "Roofer Awarded $5.1 Million Judgment," to the *Las Vegas Review Journal,* "Mutual of Omaha Caught in $5.1 Million Judgment."

The Honorable Howard McClain—presiding at the trial— was a seasoned and respected judge of the Los Angeles Superior Court. He also must have been impressed by Mutual of Omaha's testimony, because he ruled as a matter of law that the company's conduct reflected bad faith. He refused to grant Mutual a new trial or to reduce the size of the award.

After the trial, I knew my career would center full-time on insurance bad faith cases. With public attention focused increasingly on these consumer-oriented cases, more and more aggrieved policyholders approached me to do battle against the insurance industry.

In the meantime, Mutual of Omaha appealed the case all the way to the California Supreme Court. The entire appeal took almost five years, but was worth waiting for. Trial results do not set legal precedents, but Supreme Court decisions do. They hand down legal principles that live on to be the guidelines for future cases. Everyone waited patiently for the Supreme Court to speak. Finally the landmark decision was handed down. Many of the legal principles I had hoped for were now going to be established law.

The Supreme Court's lengthy opinion started out by warning that insurance companies have a trust relationship with their insureds that encompasses the public interest. When an insurance company takes advantage of this special relationship, public-policy considerations support imposing punitive damages upon the company. The Supreme Court explained it this way:

> "The insurers' obligations are rooted in their status as purveyors of a vital service labeled quasi-public in nature. Suppliers of insurance services affected with a public interest must take the public interest seriously where necessary, placing it before their interest in maximizing gains and limiting disbursements . . . the obligations of good faith and fair dealing encompass qualities of decency and humanity inherent in the responsibilities of a fiduciary. Insurers hold themselves out as fiduciaries, and with the public trust must go private responsibility consonant with that trust . . . the availability of punitive damages is thus compatible with recognition of insurers' underlying public obligations and reflects an attempt to restore balance in the contractual relationship."

Thus the *Egan* case represented a clear expression by a California court that defined the scope of bad faith law. It not only addressed the parties involved in the lawsuit, but now concluded that there was a clear public interest at stake. A private citizen could file a suit to punish insurance companies for behavior that was in violation of public interest in order to protect the consuming public. This guiding legal principle has since been adopted by other states as well.

The *Egan* decision was a far-reaching decision which touched many aspects of the insurance business. *Egan* was the first Supreme Court decision to hold an insurance company guilty of bad faith if it fails to investigate the policyholder's claim adequately. As you have seen from the Egan trial, Mutual did a miserable, one-sided job of investigating his claim. The California Supreme Court pointed out:

> "The insured in a contract like the one before us does not seek to obtain a commercial advantage by purchasing the policy—rather, he seeks protection against calamity. . . . The purchase of such insurance is to provide funds during periods when the ordinary source of the insured's income—his earnings—had stopped. The purchase of such insurance provides peace of mind and security in the event the insured is unable to work. . . . To protect these interests it is essential that an insurer fully inquire into possible bases that might support the insured's claim."

The court went on to hold squarely that:

> "An insurer cannot reasonably and in good faith deny payments to its insureds without thoroughly investigating the foundation of its denial."

Michael Egan opened the door for consumers and made it easier for them to bring their insurance companies to court. The case helps consumers obtain favorable verdicts not just for their claims, but for damages suffered because of mental distress and for punitive damages. The standard of reasonableness is now applied, and a company's entire investigatory process is held up for scrutiny. Was the investigation adequate? Was it thorough? Above all, was it fair?

The court really pointed out a very simple proposition, one that should have been obvious: insurance companies take premiums from their policyholders to protect them and they ought to act like protectors. For the past 100 years the problem has been that once a person files a claim, he is treated more like an adversary than like someone in need of protection.

During the trial, Mutual of Omaha argued that the corporation could not be punished for the acts of its agents and employees—if those agents were low-level employees who were not part of management. The company maintained that a claims adjuster may do something stupid or even wrong, yet the company should not be punished for his errant behavior.

The Supreme Court disagreed. An insurance corporation is liable for the actions of claim adjusters. The court pointed out that, from Egan's standpoint, the actions of the claim adjusters were the actions of Mutual of Omaha. Claim adjusters manage the most crucial aspects of the corporation's relationship with its policyholders. Finally, the court found that Mutual of Omaha should not be allowed to insulate itself from liability by giving an employee a non-managerial title and then allowing him to make crucial policy decisions.

The decision resulted in yet another important legal precedent. The court said that policyholders were not limited to damages at the time their cases came to trial, but that they could also receive future damages—such as future benefits payable under the insurance policies for future mental distress, in an amount which the jury determines to be reasonable.

For example, at the time that Egan's case came to trial, his disability insurance policy would have paid him only a couple of thousand dollars up to that date. Yet, if he were to receive the benefits for his entire lifetime, those benefits could reasonably have been calculated at $46,600. The jury found the entire amount due and payable at once because of Mutual of Omaha's bad faith, and awarded the entire $46,000 as well as $78,000 in emotional distress, some of which had been suffered in the past and some which still would be suffered in the future.

After giving Egan and the public at large such a tremendous victory by setting forth great legal precedents, the court handed Mutual of Omaha a bone. It determined that the $5 million in punitive damages was too severe and ordered a retrial on this single issue so that another jury could determine what an appropriate punishment might be. Thus, for Michael Egan, the battle wasn't over after ten years of fighting. Fortunately, just before the retrial, Mutual of Omaha agreed to a settlement to avoid the second trial. They insisted that the details of the settlement be kept confidential, and the court file was sealed. However, in signing the confidentiality agreement, I modified it to make sure I reserved for myself the right to recount my personal recollections about the case and trial.

The legal precedent created by the Egan case lives on and has given much-needed help to those who have followed Egan, by opening up the doors of justice to abused policyholders.

CHAPTER 6

Denial of Small Medical Claim Brings Large Settlement for Senior Citizen

Case Study: *Norman v. Colonial Penn*

Elmer Norman walked into my office wearing a homemade hearing aid. The slender elderly man had made his hearing aid by connecting stereo headphones to a box hooked to his belt. To ask questions, I had to speak through a microphone plugged into Elmer's device. He was a most unforgettable character with a $48 gripe.

Elmer told me how Colonial Penn Franklin took advantage of him by refusing to pay a $48 claim. The company had refused to pay for his medicine and a hearing test. Insurance claims adjusters argued that the policy excluded the test as well as Elmer's prescription for medicine. Though Colonial Penn concluded eventually that it should have paid for the prescription, the company refused to admit any bad faith in denying Elmer's claim for a hearing test.

I joined Elmer in his $48 battle against the Colonial Penn

Franklin Insurance Company. I never dreamed, though, that Elmer's case would become one of the greatest David and Goliath legal battles of my career.

Court congestion in California often results in months—sometimes years—of waiting before a trial can be set. Sometimes new facts emerge, and often memories fade. As the trial date neared, Colonial Penn attorneys wanted an updated deposition. They hoped to reassure themselves that they had missed nothing. The deposition gave them more than they bargained for.

In the deposition, Elmer rambled on, telling how his prospects for medical security had vanished and describing his various frustrations. Suddenly he forgot about his $48 claim and launched into a tirade about his benefits being reduced by a switch in policies. This was news to us and startled everyone. Elmer explained:

> "I discovered to my horror and sorrow that . . . Colonial Penn was promising the sun, moon and stars concerning improved benefits . . . [but] that in the matter of the out-of-hospital policy that what they promised as being improvements were really reductions in benefits. There was an increased deductible, new limitations on drugs . . . and a fantastic reduction for 80 percent of the allowable benefits in a certain number of categories down to only 20 percent."

Elmer's deposition made it clear that I needed to broaden his lawsuit to include the switch in policies. I amended the original documents to incorporate the charge that Colonial Penn had changed the policies fraudulently. That issue became the centerpiece of the lawsuit.

I filed the amended complaint, and new discovery proceedings began. I requested from Colonial Penn copies of all documents relevant to the policy switch. These revealed that Colonial Penn's true intention was to revise the out-of-hospital coverage in order to reduce loss ratios by 40 percent. The policy switch would save the company over $4 million in payouts per year. Interoffice memos and directives detailed revisions that would make the new plan appear similar to the old.

The most damaging company memos were written by Daniel Gross, president of several of Colonial Penn's subsidiaries, and Richard Saltzman, then a Colonial Penn Franklin vice-president.

The Gross memo—sent to company executives—summarized the plan as follows:

> "We are attempting to reduce claim payments by 40 percent. . . . We propose two basic changes which . . . involve reducing the amount paid on medical supplies, X-rays, and laboratory tests (which are paid under Medicare) to 20 percent of eligible expenses and establishing a separate drug deductible."

Saltzman's directive told the person responsible for making document changes:

> "This plan is going to be totally revised to incorporate certain benefit reductions in lieu of a rate increase."

Two other documents were equally damaging to Colonial Penn. These undated and unsigned memos, one handwritten, explained why the company was doing what it was doing and what the objectives were.

The second of these two, a typewritten list of objectives, summarized things nicely:

Objectives of Revision

1. *Reduce claims cost by 40 percent* [emphasis added].
2. Permit elimination of pre-existing condition exclusion.
3. Limit future claim cost inflation.
4. Prevent drug benefit dominance.
5. Minimize variety in coinsurance amounts.
6. *Appear similar to current plan* [emphasis added].

My enthusiasm for the case increased. In a gesture of friendship and in an atmosphere of excitement, I invited Richard Ben-Veniste, the former Watergate prosecutor, to join me in court. Now in private practice, he and I had cultivated a friendship for some time. Interested in bad faith cases, he was anxious to help me prove one.

Ben-Veniste was a great help in keeping Elmer on track during the trial's first phase. In one session I had Elmer under direct examination, trying to direct him to tell his story in a chronological and coherent fashion. The task did not come easily, since he tended to ramble a bit and stray off the point. I did not mind this occasionally, for it constituted part of Elmer's character. But, if Elmer rambled too much, it would definitely hurt his case. The jury might think he lacked the capacity to think clearly. At one point in his testimony, when his rambling became excessive, I called a recess so I could talk to him.

Elmer remained on the witness stand with his earphones covering his ears. After the courtroom emptied, I picked up the little microphone hanging from his side. Calmly I told him to stick to the point. Simply answer questions without elaborating, I said. Elmer did not understand, he was frustrated, he repeatedly asked me why. With little recess time left, I had no time to explain why. My frustration grew as the seconds ticked by.

Finally, Ben-Veniste grabbed the microphone from me and

asked Elmer, "Do you want to know why?" and Elmer nodded his head. Ben-Veniste then raised his voice and shouted into the microphone, "Because unless you stick to the point, you're going to lose the fucking case!" I knew he had gotten through when I saw a broad smile return to Elmer's face. From that point on, we had no trouble with rambling.

I did not want to focus on the deception from the switch in policies at the beginning of the trial; this issue would come in due time. First I wanted the jury to understand Elmer. I needed the jurors to understand the innocent nature of his relationship with Colonial Penn from the beginning.

Shernoff: "Do you recall approximately when you purchased the Colonial Penn policy that is subject to
this case?"

Norman: "When I first purchased it? Oh, yes. [Nine years
ago.]"

Q. "How did it come about that you heard about
these policies?"

A. "I presume that it was due to my mother. She had
already been a member of AARP [the American
Association of Retired Persons] and was already
insured. And she had been a bad, chronic invalid
and I used to take care of her accounts. Either they
put me on the mailing list that way or else I just got
it as a matter of advertising, solicitation through
the mail."

Elmer was wary of Colonial Penn because his mother had trouble with AARP-related health insurance. Despite his mother's problems with coverage, he separated the insurance carrier and the association mentally. He believed AARP devoted itself to the well-being of older people. When he joined AARP, the group was 11 years old and its membership had grown by half a million people per year. Later, AARP's membership increased dramatically, at the rate of one million per year.

Elmer had no reason to believe that AARP would permit a deception against its membership—certainly not by the insurance company that held AARP's endorsement. The insurance company had an exclusive right to solicit members' business, to advertise in *Modern Maturity*—the association's bimonthly magazine—and to mail its advertising and solicitation letters under AARP's nonprofit mailing status. Colonial Penn had been an integral part of AARP's formation, and AARP had nurtured Colonial Penn. This relationship was a matter of pride to AARP members.

Because of his faith in AARP, Elmer bought health insurance from Colonial Penn to supplement his limited Medicare coverage. He assumed that Colonial Penn's foot-dragging in his mother's case was endemic to the insurance business. And, if AARP said the health insurance policy was the best buy for several hundred thousand older American citizens, it was bound to be good for him. With this background, I began to discuss his claim.

Shernoff: "Mr. Norman, in December two years ago—do you recall having an ear infection in your inner ear?"

Norman: "Yes. About the middle of December."

Q. "Do you recall what type of treatment you received for your ear problem?"

A. "Yes. I had a culture test. I had X-rays. I had audio-diagnostic services and prescriptions."

Q. "Did you then put in a claim for the payment of those services with Colonial Penn?"

A. "Oh, yes."

Q. "Is that the first time you had a claim under that policy since you purchased it?"

A. "That was my very first claim."

Q. "Did you then receive a benefit check with an explanation of the benefits?"

A. "Yes."

Q. "Do you recall what your reaction was when you first received the benefit check and the explanation of the benefits?"

A. "Well, I was quite surprised because there were several different categories of benefits promised by the policy. I received partial payment only on the drugs. No payment on the audio test."

Q. "Did you write a letter to the claims department?"

A. "Yes."

The letter set forth the number and dates of visits, the treatments, the diagnoses, and the errors Colonial Penn had made in calculating reimbursements.

Shernoff: "After you sent that letter, do you recall getting a response from them?"

Norman: "Yes, I did."

Q. "Mr. Norman, does this look like the reply you received?" [I held up the letter in question.]

A. "Yes, shall I read it?"

Q. "Yes."

A. "Dear Mr. Norman:

Your letter has been referred to me for reply.

Upon careful review of the claim processed, we find that no additional benefits are due.

The complete audio evaluation performed is considered neither a diagnostic laboratory procedure, nor a diagnostic X-ray procedure; therefore, it cannot be allowed. . . .

Additionally, I found that the correct amount was allowed for prescription drugs bills you submitted. According to the *American Druggist's Blue Book* the dicloxacillin-Dynapen Capsules are not considered as prescription drugs.

Sincerely yours, Harvey Davis, Claims Department."

Q. "When you received that letter, what was your reaction?"

A. "I felt that they were in error, that they were wrong."

Q. "The letter did state they had made a careful review, is that correct?"

A. "Yes. In other words, they had seen my claim."

From his pharmacy school days, Elmer recalled that the *American Druggist's Blue Book* was nothing more than a trade journal. Elmer read federal publications and determined conclusively that a consumer could not buy Dynapen without a prescription—either under its commercial name or under the generic designation of dicloxacillin.

Elmer also described what he learned by consulting the *California Relative Value Studies.* Used by professionals to determine designations and costs, the book had convinced him that his hearing test represented a laboratory procedure. His investigation took several months.

Then I placed in evidence Elmer's next letter to Colonial Penn, in which he presented his findings. Elmer read Colonial Penn's response—sent a month later—into evidence.

Elmer: "Dear Mr. Norman:

We regret that, through a clerical error, your purchase of Dynapen was incorrectly disallowed. Our records are now being corrected and the additional benefits due for the purchase of this drug will reach you shortly. . . . Our decision not to consider hearing or vision tests as laboratory tests

> is not an arbitrary one. As your letter pointed out, the *California Relative Value Studies* lists tests of this sort as 'diagnostic procedures'; the Out-of-Hospital Medical Plan provides benefits for 'diagnostic laboratory tests.' . . .
>
>   Sincerely yours, Adrienne M. Agnew, Claims Department."

Shernoff: "What was your reaction to this letter?"

   A. "I was convinced that I was being ripped off. The . . . refusal to pay the audio test . . . really infuriated me. The whole world, I thought, understood that . . . diagnostic tests, whether in a field of medicine or mining or geology or whatever it may be, do not have to be in a vast sort of laboratory. You can carry a laboratory in your vest pocket."

Elmer explained in greater detail why the hearing test involved a diagnostic laboratory procedure. He enjoyed telling, in his homespun manner, that the claims staff at Colonial Penn reminded him of the Queen of Hearts in *Alice in Wonderland* because "They used words to mean whatever they wanted them to."

The $48 claim did not represent the case's major thrust, but I thought it worthwhile to focus the case around a small issue. I wanted the jury to see how Colonial Penn conducted business in this one instance in order to set the stage for the more serious matter: the switch in Elmer's policies.

To present details of the switch, I asked Elmer to read into evidence portions of two letters sent by Colonial Penn, which dealt specifically with the out-of-hospital health coverage. The letters were addressed to policyholders and explained why the coverage needed revision. The second letter stated in part that the new policy reflected "substantial improvements" in coverage at no additional premium.

The letters did not communicate differences between the

original and the new coverage. I intended to show the jury that Colonial Penn wanted the policyholders to believe that they were receiving a bonanza in the new coverage when, in fact, the company was substantially reducing the policy's overall worth. The two letters had been signed by Dorothy Liggett, Coordinator, AARP Insurance Plans.

Elmer had paid little attention to either letter when he received them, since he assumed that AARP looked after his interests. Elmer took the letters out of his files and reviewed them only after Colonial Penn refused to pay his medical expenses.

When Colonial Penn wrote those letters, its plan was actually to reduce benefits. At the same time, the company and its subsidiaries were amassing one of the quickest fortunes in American corporate history. Revenues that year totaled $445 million. The AARP health insurance plans alone generated about $261 million in premiums the following year. Colonial Penn Group led 929 major United States corporations in profitability, with a five-year average return on capital of 33.5 percent, while Elmer Norman lived in a modest house supported by Social Security income and dwindling reserves from the sale of his family real estate.

The two Colonial Penn letters would open the door to the jury's view of a deceptive scheme. After realizing what impact the policy switch would have on the jury, I began to feel confident that I now had the key to exposing the company's practices.

My message to the jury was obvious: Colonial Penn told policyholders it was providing better benefits when, in reality, it was secretly taking them away. The documents proved that. The memos revealed that the revision aimed to reduce claims costs by 40 percent. Worse yet, the way they implemented the goal was to make the new plan appear similar to the old.

The trial lasted 14 days and produced 1,331 pages of

transcript. Of those pages, only 788 covered actual testimony from witnesses before the jury. We spent much court time arguing law, the admissibility of evidence, and the credibility of the six witnesses. The greatest strain on the proceedings, though, involved the case for the defense. Richard Castle, Colonial Penn's lawyer, attempted to argue that the two critical letters (mailed several months apart) were totally unrelated. The first letter, he claimed, informed customers that their previous policies would change. An additional revision would occur subsequently. The first letter enclosed a rider, Castle emphasized, which explained the revised coverage. The second letter, he argued, dealt with the company's new decisions, made after the first letter had been mailed. The new decisions described in the second letter were separate and apart from the revisions set forth in the earlier communications. This was a hypertechnical and confusing defense.

The second letter stated that there were "substantial improvements" in the coverage. I kept coming back to the fact that I couldn't see any "improvements." There were some added areas of coverage in the new policy but they involved medical costs arising from pregnancy, illness, or injury due to war, care in military or government hospitals, and limited coverage due to preexisting conditions.

I didn't for a second believe they would try to sell the idea to the jury that adding coverage for pregnancy or accidents while in the military would do anything for these old folks. But Castle put on a straight face and tried to defend these additions by noting that nothing prevented an older man from having a wife of childbearing age, although he did concede that the increased risk did not cost the company much. The absurdity of awarding retired people maternity benefits was not lost on the jurors. Some laughed out loud. Castle had little to say about the war-related injuries or veterans' hospital exclusions since, as we pointed out, those hospitals offered free care anyway. Nor did he have much to offer in explaining the elimination of the preexisting condition exclusion. The new "benefit" would have absolutely no meaning to Elmer or anyone else previously insured.

Howard Clark, a founder of the National Insurance Consumer Organization and former State Insurance Commissioner in South Carolina, testified that the new maternity benefits were "illusory" and benefits for war and care in military hospitals were "absolutely meaningless."

Concerning Elmer's original complaints—the carrier's refusal to pay for the Dynapen medicine and the audiogram ear test—Castle argued that anyone could make a mistake. Castle said, "That is why they have erasers on pencils." The company did pay when it discovered the Dynapen error. As for the audiogram, everyone was entitled to his own opinion, and Colonial Penn's argument had more credibility than Elmer's, said Castle. Nevertheless, he noted in closing argument, since a reasonable doubt existed, the company changed its policies regarding hearing tests and paid Elmer the $48.

The defense spent the remaining time attempting to justify Colonial Penn's internal documents. The attorneys tried to exclude evidence of Colonial Penn Group's net worth, hoping to minimize possible punitive damages. The parent company, Colonial Penn Group, owned some dozen subsidiaries, including Colonial Penn Franklin. Castle failed on the first count and succeeded only partially on the second.

Castle then struggled, first to keep the documents from being admitted as evidence, and next to keep parts of the documents from entering the record. Castle's attempts to prevent admission of the documents failed and the trial drew to a close. Castle decided to pursue a new tactic. Even if the documents did say what they said, surely they did not intend to deceive. Instead, the documents tried innocently to provide the best solution for thousands of elderly citizens. In his closing argument, Castle tried to convince the jury in this way:

> "But if in fact Colonial Penn Franklin was devious, fraudulent, was dishonest, you would never have seen those documents, ladies and gentlemen. . . . Now, if there were any documents that looked bad, Colonial Penn Franklin could have destroyed the documents or just not produced them. There is no way Mr. Shernoff would know, no way you would know. These are the documents that came out of the bowels of the old records of Colonial Penn Franklin."

The implication that it is easy and probably common for litigants to break the laws of discovery when it suits them is certainly a strange argument for a lawyer attempting to defend his client's honor in a closing argument. I handled that point in the following way:

> "How silly. How silly. How dumb does he think people are? We are in a lawsuit now. When you are talking about producing documents in a lawsuit and you . . . lie under oath, that is perjury. And if you don't produce something that is supposed to be produced in a lawsuit, you can be held in contempt of court.
>
> And look at all the important people on these documents. The president of the company, all these executives. Now, they may not be too concerned about turning over documents [that could lead to] a punitive damage award. But if they don't turn over documents, and somebody finds out about it later, they go down the road to the other country club, the

one that has got bars on it. That is why we got those
documents. Those important people didn't want to
run the risk of not turning them over, and I don't
blame them."

Having failed to keep the damaging memos out of evidence, Castle's next effort was to minimize Colonial Penn
Franklin's wealth and to suppress all information about Colonial Penn Franklin's profits. The court compromised on the
issue, refusing to allow us to present to the jury the parent
company's net worth. We were permitted to enter testimony
that revealed Colonial Penn Franklin's profits, generated by
health insurance, and how the company funneled those
profits up to Colonial Penn Group.

Castle used Robert Saltzman, the executive vice-president
of Colonial Penn Franklin and an officer of Colonial Penn
Group, to rationalize the revisions. Directed by Castle's questions, Saltzman testified that Colonial Penn Franklin was
losing money on the out-of-hospital plan.

In our cross-examination, we refuted Saltzman's testimony
and proved that the company's profits on health insurance
totaled nearly $26 million. Colonial Penn's financial manipu-
lation among the group's companies created an illusion that
profits were low. We showed that the company not only
generated a handsome profit from all the health plans, but
that the profits increased steadily. We asked, why should the
company feel it was necessary to change the one policy, when
it was doing so well overall?

We based our closing argument on ordinary logic. It
helped return Elmer to the jury's consciousness. I stressed
how Colonial Penn had repeatedly discounted his claims.
First they searched a book under the general name of a drug,
and when the book explicitly said, "look under the brand
name," they didn't do it. Instead, the company said that the
drug wasn't listed as a prescription drug. That's tantamount,

I said, to looking in the Yellow Pages for a lawyer and then deciding none existed in your area because under "lawyers" the book says "see attorneys."

I had to explain the significance of those words "appear similar to current plan." I was eager, but I also had to avoid the evangelism that sometimes overcomes a closing argument.

> "Those words are plain English. You don't have to be a Philadelphia lawyer to figure out what they mean. . . . In other words, let's give it an appearance that is similar."

Castle contended that it would have been misleading had Colonial Penn told its customers that 40 percent of the benefits were being taken away because this wasn't true for everyone: some would lose more and some less. My response was:

> "If the insurance company couldn't find a way to tell the truth, it is a sad state of affairs as far as insurance practices [go]. They don't have to say it is going to be exactly a 40 percent reduction. All they have to do is be fair. Disclose. They could say something like 'the plan is going to be revised and in the aggregate it is going to be a 40 percent reduction; some people might get more, some people might get less, but on average it will be 40 percent. . . .'
>
> "I believe in a decent profit. But I don't believe in an excessive profit, especially when you're dealing with old folks.
>
> "I believe in telling them the truth, the whole truth, not half the truth, and not making a bunch of explanations why you can't tell the truth.
>
> "It is up to you, ladies and gentlemen; in the last analysis you are the ones that are going to decide, did they play fair with these elderly people?"

I reminded the jury of those two letters to illustrate just how Colonial Penn Franklin did business with AARP.

> "They have [the letters] signed by Dorothy Liggett, Coordinator of AARP Insurance Plans. We know that she has no connection with AARP whatsoever. She is not even a member of AARP. She works as a full-time employee of National Association Plans, which is a wholly owned subsidiary of Colonial Penn Group, which owns the company involved in this lawsuit.
>
> "Now if you get a letter from AARP Insurance Plans, with the AARP seal, signed by Dorothy Liggett, Coordinator of AARP Insurance Plans, do you think you have the right to conclude that maybe this letter is coming from AARP and they knew of this letter and approved of what was going on?"

Testimony during trial, I pointed out, proved that Liggett had nothing to do with the decision to revise the insurance plan. She also had no idea why the company made the revisions. I reminded the jury that AARP Insurance Plans was a nonexistent entity, nothing more than a letterhead.

Liggett's deposition testimony had shown that she and her title were tools for Colonial Penn.

Shernoff: "As I understand it, you had nothing to do with the preparation of these form letters?"

Liggett: "That's right."

Q. "And your signature then was placed [by stamp] on the form letter which went out to the various insureds. Is that correct?"

A. "That's correct."

Q. "Were you told at the time that your signature was affixed to these letters that the purpose of the

> change in the out-of-hospital plan was to reduce
> payouts by 40 percent?"
> A. "No, I wasn't."

I ended my argument by explaining the value of punitive
damage awards and the several ways these awards can be
viewed. Was it punishment at all, in fact, just to take back the
money, the ill-gotten gains, that didn't belong to the company
to begin with?

> "When we talk about punishment in cases involv-
> ing fraud, malice, and oppression, all we are really
> talking about is a fine, a penalty."

I told the jury that what Colonial Penn understood best was
money.

> "[Let's] send them a legal message that has a
> dollar sign on it and tell them, 'This isn't a way you
> treat elderly people. If you're going to sell insurance
> to old people and you're going to make millions and
> millions of dollars, year after year, you better be fair
> to them. Because if you're not fair and you start to cut
> corners, and you [commit] fraud, an American jury
> is going to tell you to watch your step.' "

Castle's closing argument concentrated on absolving Colonial Penn Franklin from charges of malice, fraud, and oppression and on minimizing the company's profits.

The testimony portion of the trial ended and the jury
commenced deliberations.

Elmer, who had attended most sessions of the trial, stayed
away. I told him we would call him when the verdict came in.

The morning there was a verdict, I called Elmer just before
I left for the courthouse. Elmer's car broke down twice on the

way from Azusa to Pomona. At 10:20 A.M. the proceedings began, even though Elmer was stranded on the freeway.

> The Court: "In the case of Norman versus Colonial Penn, Mr. Noble [the jury foreman], I understand the jury has reached a verdict."
>
> The Foreman: "Yes, they have, your Honor."
>
> The Court: "Will you hand it to the bailiff? The record will reflect the presence of counsel and the jury panel and the alternate."

The Clerk read the following verdict:

> "We, the jury, find for the plaintiff, Elmer Norman, and against the defendant, Colonial Penn Franklin Insurance Company, and assess damages as follows:
>   Compensatory damages, $70,000.
>   Punitive damages, $4,500,000."

All the blood drained from Castle's face when the verdict was read. At his request, the court polled the jury. The verdict was unanimous. Castle was always a gentleman, and I remember him as being very gracious. He talked to the jurors and asked them what had gone wrong, and then he made a gentlemanly exit.

About this time, Elmer arrived at the courthouse. He remembers it this way:

> "I came into the courthouse and everybody was still there. The outstanding thing in my mind is how Bill turned around and spied me and he took my hand and shook it and he smiled. Then I heard him say I won and the verdict was four-and-a-half-million dollars. I was stunned. I went out into the hallway and there was all this buzzing and talking. I started to

thank the jurors for giving the case such attention and
then the amazing thing was that they thanked me for
bringing it to their attention."

Perhaps more than any other case, the verdict demonstrated that no matter how small or infirm a person is, our
system of justice allows anyone to make a difference—if he
or she is right, and if he or she is persistent. Thanks to Elmer
Norman, insurance companies *should* now think long and
hard about taking advantage of older policyholders.

CHAPTER 7

Hospital Insurance—Make Sure You Know What You Are Buying

Case Study: *Warren v. Colonial Penn*

Unfortunately, Colonial Penn Franklin did not learn a good lesson from the Norman case. I recently had another tangle with them, which resulted in a jury assessing a punitive damage award of $4 million against them. This case involved hospital indemnity policies that we all see advertised on TV. It pays so much a day (like $50) for every day one is hospitalized. My client, Julius Warren, was hospitalized for about 400 days, in a Veterans Administration hospital, after being severely injured in an auto accident. He was completely bedridden and had over 40 broken bones. It took this entire time of hospitalization just to get him back on his feet again. Colonial Penn Franklin paid for only 40 days of this hospitalization, rather than the 400 days. They claimed the balance of the hospitalization was not medically necessary. Colonial Penn Franklin made this decision without consulting the treating physician or examining Mr. Warren. A registered nurse at their home office simply looked at a portion of the hospital records and decided that most of the hospitalization was not medically necessary. They used a definition of "medically necessary" that we believed was different from the definition contained within the insurance policy. The jury awarded Mr. Warren his insurance benefits, which amounted to $102,000, and also assessed Colonial Penn Franklin a huge punitive damage penalty.

The point of this case is that people should be very suspect of the hospital indemnity policies that are advertised on TV, sometimes by movie stars. One has to be able to understand the fine print because there are many traps for the unsuspecting. For example, many times skilled nursing facilities, rehabilitation facilities, convalescent homes, extended-care facilities, and other related entities are excluded from the definition of "hospital." Therefore, it sounds as if you'll get a lot of money for every day you are in the hospital, but in most cases, people are in an acute hospital for only a short period of time and then transferred to other facilities. Once this transfer takes place, you don't get paid anymore because it does not meet the definition of "hospital." Also, as in the Warren case, it is important who is going to make the decision of whether a hospitalization is medically necessary. If that decision is left to the insurance company, they may cut you off a lot sooner, even though your treating physician feels that hospitalization is necessary.

The Warren verdict was one of the first cases to attack the abuses inherent in the hospital indemnity policy. These policies are generally sold to the elderly as Medicare supplements.

These cases point to one inescapable conclusion. The elderly who buy this type of insurance must be very careful to know what they are buying. Stay away from insurance companies and policies which do not deliver what the advertising implies is being sold.

CHAPTER 8

Who Has the Right to Determine the Necessity of Medical Treatment? Your Doctor or Your Insurance Company?

Case Study: *Sarchett v. Blue Shield*

For a lot of people, fighting the blues means suing Blue Shield or Blue Cross to get their medical bills paid. In many of these cases, we've been able to win significant victories for embattled Blues policyholders.

Most Blue Cross and Blue Shield policyholders don't know that, even if their doctor orders hospitalization, medical advisers hired by these companies may decide after the fact that the doctors were wrong. When this happens, hospital patients whose condition appeared life-threatening to their doctor at the time of treatment may come away from the hospital with a clean bill of health and a huge bill for services rendered.

John Sarchett was one person who slugged it out with the Blues. His story is a typical yet startling example of the

Monday-morning quarterbacking that goes on in Blue health-plan huddles. It's a kind of second-guessing that the policyholder has little chance to discover, since there is usually nothing written in the insurance policy explaining this procedure, commonly referred to as a "retrospective review." Policyholders are not told their doctor-ordered care is subject to later review by the plans' doctors and administrators.

John Sarchett had been healthy most of his 57 years. Sarchett rarely missed a day as director of the Los Angeles County Probation Department. When he began having severe stomach and mid-back pain, he let several weeks go by before general weakness forced him to consult Dr. Bruce Van Vranken, his family physician. Dr. Van Vranken examined him but made no diagnosis. He ran some tests and asked John to return if things took a turn for the worse. John went back to his doctor a few days later. Dr. Van Vranken ordered John to check in at Foothill Presbyterian Hospital in Glendora, California. Tests were run while nurses and doctors attended to John and tried to relieve his pain. The tests turned up anemia and a low white blood cell count. John spent three days in the hospital before his condition improved enough for him to go home. Dr. Van Vranken concluded that John's problem may have been a small bleeding ulcer which simply stopped bleeding.

Eventually John received a $1,116 bill from the hospital, which he had expected his Blue Shield health plan to pay. Blue Shield refused to pay, claiming that John's hospitalization was not medically necessary. Blue Shield administrators had simply overruled the judgment of the attending physician without ever examining the patient. They said they reviewed the hospital records and, in their opinion, John should have been treated as an outpatient. John was left holding the bag, punished for obeying his doctor's orders.

The key question in the case of *John Sarchett v. Blue Shield* is: who should make the determination that hospitalization is necessary? John Sarchett said it should be his treating doctor. Blue Shield maintained adamantly that it has the right to make a retrospective review of hospital records and reverse the treating doctor's findings.

The scenario was familiar to me, and I knew it was familiar to a significant number of Blue Shield policyholders. I also knew that it would take a court case to change Blue Shield's procedures. We took John's case, hoping that a victory would force Blue Shield to change its ways.

In order to resolve the issues quickly, we agreed to arbitrate the matter with Blue Shield. The American Arbitration Association handled the case. At the hearing we presented our evidence, including letters exchanged between Dr. Van Vranken, Blue Shield, and John Sarchett. A key letter for the case was written by Dr. Van Vranken to Blue Shield. It said:

> "It is my understanding that Mr. Sarchett was denied coverage for hospitalization. I am writing this letter to strongly protest this action because it is my sincere belief that this hospitalization was completely justified and indeed urgently needed. This patient was seen in my office the day of his hospitalization feeling very weak, with a very marked anemia and many other symptoms which in my mind were indeed in need of immediate care.
>
> ". . . It is my sincere professional opinion that immediate hospitalization was indicated for the patient's treatment and welfare as well as for further diagnostic evaluation. It is my contention that I would have been professionally negligent if I had failed to initiate the above medical procedures as I did. I strongly protest the action of denying his claims and beseech you to grant his hospitalization as he has requested."

We also called Dr. Jack Japenga, the head of the Foothill Presbyterian Hospital utilization review committee, a standard hospital committee that reviews admissions and other hospital procedures. He told the arbitrator that the hospital committee found John Sarchett's admission fully justified.

Blue Shield's primary defense was based upon its own doctors' review of John's hospital charts after the fact. Testifying for Blue Shield was Dr. Robert Wolf, a retired physician hired by the insurance plan to review medical charts to determine questions of medical necessity. Wolf maintained that John's hospital admission was unjustified.

Three years after the disputed hospitalization, the arbitrator ordered Blue Shield to pay the $1,116 hospital bill and awarded John $12,000 in damages for mental and emotional distress. Most significantly, the arbitrator ordered Blue Shield to pay $300,000 in punitive damages. The $313,116 verdict represented a tremendous victory for John and for others who had similar conflicts with the Blues.

Usually an arbitration award ends the matter quickly, because they are rarely appealed. However, Blue Shield was not going to take this award lying down. It would either have to revamp its entire method of claims review or risk a punitive-damage award whenever a claim was denied based on hindsight. Blue Shield decided to attack the punitive-damage award. The arbitration award was set aside by a trial court on a technicality because Blue Shield argued that it had been denied the right to call a second doctor to testify during the arbitration hearing.

I thought the decision to throw out the arbitration was wrong. Additional medical information would have made no difference; another Blue Shield doctor simply would have echoed Dr. Wolf's testimony. We were left with only one thing to do: try the case all over again. This time I wanted it in front of a jury, while Blue Shield wanted another arbitration. I was successful, and the stage was set for a jury trial.

My strategy was to present the court with a very strong trial memorandum. I wanted the judge to understand that significant public-interest issues were involved and to support the importance of the punitive-damage aspect. Large punitive awards have a direct bearing on the public because they cause big companies to modify their behavior.

We also wanted to make clear to the judge that we thought Blue Shield would try to confuse the issues and would base its case on medical testimony gathered from an after-the-fact review of hospital records. The testimony would, of course, conclude that the hospitalization was unnecessary. This was not the issue. We knew there could be differences of opinion; anyone can find doctors who will disagree. Blue Shield hired doctors to conduct a hindsight review of a hospital chart for the sole purpose of reducing claims expense and not to treat patients on the spot for their physical suffering.

On the day of the trial we handed the court our lengthy trial document setting forth our positions. We said, in part:

> "This case will decide whether Blue Shield's practice, as described herein, violates its duty of good faith and fair dealing owed to its policyholder. The resolution of this case will have a tremendous impact on thousands of other policyholders who find themselves in similar situations."

The case was tried in front of a jury with the Honorable William McVittie presiding. My opponent was Bill Sturgeon, a good, tough lawyer whom I had faced before in court. To make it a little bit tougher, he brought along Tom French, the lawyer who had handled the arbitration hearing. Sturgeon called Tom French his "brains."

We presented our case first, as is customary in civil actions. John, the patient, was the first witness. He was articulate and impressive. His wife, Evelyn, a registered nurse, testified next and gave a good account of the concern she had for her husband when he became sick. Dr. Van Vranken also proved to be an impressive witness. He had been a member physician of Blue Shield for 20 years, and his medical competence had never been questioned by the health plan.

We also called two doctors from Foothill Presbyterian's utilization review committee. Drs. Jack Japenga and John Camp testified that their committee had reviewed the records thoroughly and had concluded repeatedly that John Sarchett's hospital admission was justified. They told the jury that they had written to Blue Shield of their decision several times.

Our testimony ended with the appearance of Dr. Edward Zalta, then president of the Southern California Physicians Council and a former president of the Los Angeles County Medical Association. On the witness stand, Dr. Zalta gave his opinion of the adequacy of Blue Shield's review, commenting:

> "This type of review would be very unfair to the patient, be very unfair to the physician who is responsible for admitting the patient to the hospital, and would do no more than satisfy the self-interest of the insurance company, Blue Shield."

Blue Shield's review was based on the hospital chart alone, not on the doctor's office chart. Blue Shield had not contacted Dr. Van Vranken before it decided to refuse payment, and did not know John's medical history. Dr. Zalta gave his opinion:

> "It is impossible to do justice to any review of a hospitalization unless one has first contacted and ascertained from the treating physician his reasons for hospitalization."

I then pursued what Blue Shield did after its initial refusal to pay John's hospital bill. To begin with, the company received a comprehensive letter from Dr. Van Vranken, explaining why he had ordered John's hospital admission.

When questioned, Dr. Zalta commented:

"I felt that that review, after having received Dr. Van Vranken's thorough letter, in which he stated in detail the reason for hospitalization, was extremely unfair to the patient because they again denied reimbursement for a justified hospitalization."

I asked Dr. Zalta his opinion of Blue Shield's general practice of retrospective chart review to deny claims.

Shernoff: "And what is your opinion of the retrospective chart review?"

Zalta: "I consider retrospective chart review, which means going back after the fact and trying to reconstruct what happened on an admission some time before, as being extremely inadequate at best. [It punishes] the patient [and is] unfair to the physician because you are using something after the fact, what we call in retrospect. I feel that in almost all cases it is self-serving to the insurance company."

Later on in his testimony, Dr. Zalta expressed it even more strongly.

Shernoff: "Doctor, what is your opinion of Blue Shield's review process in this case?"

After we had rested our case, Blue Shield stuck to the game plan I had predicted. They called a seemingly endless series of doctors to buttress their decision that John Sarchett's hospitalization—based upon a review of the hospital chart—was not necessary.

When both sides were finished, I decided to ask the court to rule, as a matter of law, that Blue Shield violated its duty of good faith and fair dealing. Factual determinations—the who-what-when-where questions—are for the jury to determine, but legal determinations—those questions where the law applies to undisputed facts—are for the judge. The question of who has the right to determine whether a patient should be hospitalized appeared to me to be a legal matter. I felt most strongly that the answer had to be the treating doctor. It was simple logic that the person best able to treat the patient was the doctor who examined him. I thought that the only way Blue Shield could reserve the right to second-guess the treating doctor would be to write such a provision in their policies, and I knew, as did everyone else, that there was no such provision in the policies. Blue Shield wouldn't want such language in their policies; otherwise it would not be able to sell them.

After hearing arguments and reviewing legal authorities, Judge McVittie made the following ruling:

"Most people who have such health insurance coverage would assume that they are required to rely on the judgment of their physician when they go to the hospital.

"I note that when Blue Shield advertises, they point out a feature of their plan is the choice of member physicians, yet nowhere in a Blue Shield brochure is it pointed out that those who choose the plan may not rely on their own physician's judgment in determining whether or not their coverage applies.

"In the instant case there is a classic case of conflicting medical judgment: the judgment of Dr. Van Vranken versus that of Dr. Wolf. The decision was resolved here by Blue Shield in favor of its own economic interest to the detriment of the interest of its insured.

"I appreciate the fact that an organization such as Blue Shield must control its costs, but the costs of the plan should not be kept competitive with other plans through denial of benefits that are expected, and this type of practice only promotes the continued deception of the public where they are called upon to make a critical choice between competing health plans. Therefore, as matter of law, the practice of Blue Shield in disagreeing with the judgment of the treating physician to hospitalize his patient solely on the basis of retrospective review of hospital files is found to be a violation of the duty of good faith and fair dealing."

This was a great legal victory. The only remaining question for the jury would be the matter of damages. The court's ruling did not entitle us automatically to punitive damages. The standard for awarding punitive damages is more rigid than the standard for determining bad faith. I would have to convince the jury that Blue Shield disregarded John Sarchett's rights consciously. The thrust of my argument was simple:

". . . Basically, Dr. Van Vranken thought his patient was dying and he did what a good doctor should do: put him in the hospital and find out what's wrong with him. Dr. Van Vranken thought he would have been guilty of malpractice had he not done that, and I agree with him.

". . . Dr. Wolf did not see the patient, did not talk to the doctor, did not consult with the doctor, only looked at the hospital records, only looked at the chart, and he made a decision that the patient wasn't sufficiently ill to be in the hospital. Now, that's what we say is a conscious disregard of the patient's rights."

I took about 45 minutes to argue the case. Then Sturgeon got up and talked to the jury for over an hour. He laboriously went over each piece of correspondence, all of the hospital charts, all the testimony, in an obvious attempt to have the jury turn its attention away from the main point. Sturgeon wanted to demonstrate to the jury that Blue Shield's review was the best they could do under the circumstances.

The jury *did* decide to punish Blue Shield. John Sarchett was awarded $100,000: $20,000 for mental distress and $80,000 in punitive damages. Although the award was not as large as I had hoped for, a significant issue was resolved. Now maybe Blue Shield would be forced to change its ways.

I thought that Blue Shield might decide to pay the judgment. After all, this was the second time the company had tried the same issue and lost. However, Blue Shield decided to appeal. For the appeal, we brought into the case Leonard Sacks, a brilliant legal writer and scholar, who assists us in all our appeals. The appeal took almost three years. It seemed like an eternity. Finally, the California Supreme Court ruled that coverage would be afforded to a policyholder, such as Sarchett, unless the insurance company could prove that the treating physician's judgment was plainly unreasonable or contrary to good medical practice. In short, an insurance company will not be able to overrule judgments of treating doctors on questions of medical necessity, unless it has evidence demonstrating that the doctor is doing something contrary to good medical practice. After a long legal struggle, the Sarchett case produced valuable law in situations where insurance companies overrule judgments of treating physicians.

However, in John's case, the judge ruled Blue Shield was guilty of bad faith and the California Supreme Court held that this should have been for the jury to decide. So they ordered another trial. For John, this meant going back to trial for the third time on his original $1,200 hospital bill. The case was now almost ten years old. Both John and I were getting tired of it. It was like going to see a movie for the third time. We decided that an out-of-court settlement would be appropriate since the law now had been established. So, John ended up taking a favorable out-of-court settlement that required Blue Shield to pay over 30 times the amount of the original hospital bill.

CHAPTER 9

A Dying Woman Fights for Her Rights to Nursing Care Coverage

Case Study: *Visconti v. Blue Cross*

The lesson of this case was brought home forcibly in the words of Barbara Visconti, who said, "It's a shame. We are victims because we allow ourselves to be victims."

This woman, dying of heart disease at the age of 53, spoke those words to me near the end of her life. She died before her victory against Blue Cross of California, but she fought a courageous battle up to the end.

When she was hospitalized, her Blue Cross major medical policy was the one bit of comfort she had, after learning that she was suffering from severe cardiomyopathy. There was no cure for this disease that would swell her heart muscles and eventually kill her.

She spent several weeks in the hospital in San Diego, California, and was finally released with the recommendation that she arrange for skilled nursing care at home. The side effects and the toxicity of the drugs she took required constant monitoring. She assumed that the $1,400 weekly

cost for round-the-clock care would be paid by her Blue
Cross major medical health plan. Her son and daughter-in-
law, Steve and Naomi Lesberg, checked with Barbara's Blue
Cross agent, who assured them the policy would cover the
home nursing care. All that would be required, said the
agent, was a letter from her doctor explaining that the skilled
care was essential to Barbara's health and well-being.

Her doctor wrote the required letter, and Barbara submitted the nursing care bills to Blue Cross for payment. Indeed,
five months of bills were submitted to the health plan office
before Blue Cross wrote Barbara and told her that the company would not pay the bills, any of them. In the interim,
she had taken money from her savings account to pay the
nurses.

After the denial, the Lesbergs panicked. They contacted
someone in the San Diego office, who told them to get a more
definitive letter from Barbara's doctor. Her cardiologist, Mar-
shall Franklin, wrote Blue Cross, affirming that "Barbara
cannot exist outside a hospital atmosphere without skilled
nursing help at home."

Blue Cross chose to disbelieve Dr. Franklin's clearly stated
opinion and instead decided that the care Barbara received at
home was "custodial" care rather than "skilled" care. Barbara's policy did not cover "custodial" nursing. The company then concluded her expenses were not eligible for Blue
Cross payments.

A custodial nurse is licensed to bathe and feed patients
and, in general, to keep them comfortable. Skilled care
nurses are licensed to do all of the custodial functions plus
give injections, administer medicines, help evaluate symp-
toms—in general, assist in treating the patient. There was no
clear definition of skilled or custodial care in Barbara's insurance policy, and we believed that Blue Cross was acting in its
own interest by refusing to pay for Barbara's care.

Within eight months, Barbara had run out of savings. She

owed over $20,000 to her nurses, who declared they could no longer work without being paid. The Lesbergs came to the rescue by converting their garage into a makeshift hospital. Naomi Lesberg nursed her mother-in-law in the best way she knew how. Despite Barbara's weak and declining health, she knew that Blue Cross was denying money that was rightfully hers. She was very angry and she told her daughter-in-law she wanted to fight.

We filed the lawsuit soon after Barbara and her family told us their sad story. The complaint read like an indictment.

"Blue Cross refused to pay the nursing bills after advising Barbara they would be covered.

"Blue Cross refused to speak to Barbara about her claim.

"Blue Cross refused to meet with Barbara personally for the purpose of determining her condition.

"Blue Cross consciously disregarded the opinion of Barbara's treating doctors that skilled nursing care was essential to her health and comfort.

"Blue Cross refused to discuss Barbara's condition with her doctors.

"Blue Cross failed to obtain Barbara's medical and hospital records.

"Blue Cross refused to discuss the nature of the skilled nursing care with the skilled nurses who worked at Barbara's home for six months.

"Blue Cross had unqualified claims people make medical decisions about Barbara's need for skilled care.

"Blue Cross consciously disregarded Barbara's medical needs."

The complaint also included information gleaned from letters back and forth between the family and Blue Cross. We pointed out that eventually the family had engaged in nothing short of begging for reimbursement.

The lawsuit was filed, but before the case came to court, Barbara Visconti died with debts and without the dignity she had sought. We vowed to continue her fight. We were infuriated by the realization that for the last months of her life she had lived in a converted garage without the skilled nursing care she required. In her conversations with us, Mrs. Visconti had said time and again that the system was wrong, that it needed bucking.

The case came up for trial about a year after Barbara's death. Under California law, it is not possible to claim damages for mental distress for persons already deceased, but the claims for medical bills and punitive damages remained valid. In fact, the case would now be concerned primarily with punitive damages. Barbara had wanted to set an example. We knew what she had suffered, and we were determined to punish Blue Cross in a big way.

We were aware that Blue Cross wasn't feeling very good about the case because shortly before the trial date, the company paid the nursing care bills—a little late for Barbara, but it was at least some acknowledgment on the company's part that she had been right.

The day before the trial was due to start, the judge called the two sides for a settlement conference. He heard both sides of the story, and he told the Blue Cross lawyers they would be in for big trouble from a jury. The company's three lawyers and a Blue Cross claims examiner seemed to take the judge's admonitions to heart, and after a relatively short time, they came to the conclusion to pay up.

We decided to accept no offer less than $400,000. The first Blue Cross offer was $100,000. We rejected it quickly. We were perfectly willing to go all the way and have a jury decide the amount. Within a couple of hours, Blue Cross agreed to $400,000.

I will never forget Barbara's courage and tenacity. She was willing to buck the Blues from her deathbed in a converted garage. She was right: we all become victims when we allow ourselves to be victimized.

CHAPTER 10

The Story of Justin's Car

Case Study: *Ingram v. Commercial Bankers Life*

Southern California is smoggy. Even healthy people have trouble breathing when the air gets really bad. It is worse for a disabled child like Justin Ingram, who was suffering from severe muscular dystrophy. When Justin's doctor told Joe and Mary, Justin's parents, that the smog was a detriment to the boy's health, they decided to leave their Pomona, California, home for the high desert city of Winchester, where the air was cleaner.

The Ingrams found their new settlement pleasant. Joe was a truck driver, and he could drive just as easily from Winchester as from Pomona. Mary enjoyed the desert community. Their only problem was the 60 miles to Kaiser Hospital in Fontana, where Justin was undergoing medical treatment. In addition to his regular treatment at Kaiser, Justin was due for a special surgical procedure and recovery follow-up that required a 100-mile trip to Children's Hospital in San Diego.

The family owned an old Plymouth that had traveled 200,000 miles and was not dependable. Joe decided to invest all their money in a down payment on a new Oldsmobile station wagon. The new wagon, called "Justin's car," was delivered three days before Justin was due for his operation in San Diego.

Justin had the operation, and his postoperative plaster cast stretched from his waist to his toes. The station wagon enabled the Ingrams to bring Justin and his wheelchair home after the operation.

When Joe Ingram bought the station wagon, he bought a credit disability policy with Commercial Bankers Life Insurance Company. This kind of insurance promises to make installment payments if a time-payment buyer becomes disabled. Joe thought that if anything happened to him, the insurance company would take over the payments, and Justin would still have the use of the new station wagon.

Soon after he bought the car, Joe injured his back. His job was heavy-duty labor, impossible for someone with a bad back.

When Joe began treatment for his back injury, he filed a claim with Commercial Bankers. Immediately the insurance company became Joe's adversary. Disputes took place over every aspect of his disability, including a proposed doctor's examination. Commercial Bankers made a couple of installment payments on the station wagon, but refused to continue unless Joe agreed to an independent medical exam. Joe had no quarrel with this request.

Although Commercial Bankers originally wanted Joe to go to a doctor two hours away in Los Angeles, they eventually agreed to Joe's request for a local doctor. Joe went to his appointment with Dr. Joseph Klein in nearby Hemet. Joe thought the examination would show Commercial Bankers that his claim was legitimate. Dr. Klein even agreed to treat Joe regularly for his back. Commercial Bankers had a different point of view.

Meanwhile, Security Pacific National Bank was getting

increasingly insistent about Joe's late car payments. The bank sent a representative out to the Ingrams' house. Joe was not home at the time, and Mary was given a good scare. Joe called the bank, and the officials assured him that no action would be taken to repossess the car without informing them beforehand. He felt sure that once Commercial Bankers saw Dr. Klein's request, the car payments would resume.

Suddenly an event took place that sent Joe flying into my office. The account that follows is Joe's own version, given when I had Joe tell his story from the witness stand three years later.

Under oath, Joe explained how he thought his problem with Commercial Bankers was about to be resolved, how things seemed to be straightening out. Then, while on errands, only *one day* after he had the conversation with the bank, he got the surprise of his life. This was the way Joe described it to the jury.

Ingram: "I was in the post office getting my mail. As I was walking out the door, a young male was in my car.

"He just started it up, and I yelled at him to get out of the car. And he saw me, and he gunned the car, jumped about an 18-inch curb.

"I went in the store, was going to call the highway patrol, the sheriff, or any law enforcement agency that I could get ahold of. . . . The highway patrol asked me if my car had been repossessed, and I said no. . . . I said it was stolen. And they asked me to call the bank who had it financed to make double sure before they picked up the guy that took the car.

"And I called the bank, and at that time they informed me that the car had been repossessed. The order had been put out the day before."

Right after the repossession, as soon as he regained his composure, Joe called Commercial Bankers to find out what was going on. I asked him to tell the jury what the insurance company said.

> "I tried to call the president and vice-president of Commercial Bankers Insurance Company person-to-person on Friday, the same day the car was taken. Whoever it was answering the phone . . . put me on hold; and then she came back and said they would contact me."

I initially learned this story from a letter Joe wrote asking for my help. It ended with these words:

> "I've never hated anyone or anything, nor have I ever been so humiliated, or embarrassed, as I was when they put me through an actual robbery, when they stole my car. I now know what it is to hate. I want revenge on Commercial Bankers in the greatest way. My limited vocabulary cannot describe the mental and physical anguish this has caused me and my family or the great burden this has put on myself, knowing my son's car has been taken from him. . . . I worked very hard to acquire my car and faithfully paid for insurance for my car payments so that my family would have certain provisions in case of an emergency. Now, even this has been stripped from my family's well-being."

When I first read this letter, I thought Commercial Bankers had made a mistake. I asked Joe to write Commercial Bankers a letter because, under California law, a person has a little time to recover repossessed property, and I thought if Joe explained what had happened, Commercial Bankers might reevaluate their position. Joe wrote the letter but got no response.

The jury sat quietly as Joe read the letter aloud, about how he'd been examined by at least five doctors, and all agreed he was disabled and no longer fit for his strenuous work. The letter described in technical detail what the doctors told Joe was happening to his spine and the treatments he required.

Before Joe had finished reading the letter, he broke down and sobbed. I asked the judge if I could finish reading Joe's letter. The judge said that would be a good idea. I turned to the jury and continued.

Shernoff: "Just recently we found out we are going to have to start taking Justin to Children's Hospital in San Diego, some 70 miles each way; and now, because you are refusing to live up to the terms of the insurance written by your company, I will have to attempt to get him there in an old Plymouth with over 200,000 miles on it.

"Our new station wagon was repossessed. . . . They put me through an actual robbery. They stole it from me while I was in the U.S. Post Office in Winchester. The police arrived and asked me to call the bank to see if it was repossessed. . . . The bank told me they repossessed my car. This whole episode was witnessed by other people, and I have never been so humiliated or embarrassed.

"Would you please reconsider my claim? I'm asking for an eight-year-old boy who is seriously ill and is in dire need of a reliable automobile.

"The bank notified me that I only have until the 23rd of this month to resolve this matter. Would you please send me your immediate reply?

"Yours very truly, Joe Ingram."

I finished reading the letter to the jury, and then I asked Joe:

Shernoff: "Mr. Ingram, did anybody from the insurance company telephone you in response to this letter?

Ingram: "No, sir, they didn't."

Q. "You did receive a letter from Commercial Bankers after you wrote this, did you not?"

A. "No, sir, I didn't."

Joe and then Mary testified that they began using the Plymouth to transport Justin. Mary said that the fumes from the Plymouth made Justin sick. One time the muffler actually caught fire and burned a hole through the floor. Their testimony showed that these were bad times for the family. Desperately in need of money to pay debts and live, Joe eventually filed for bankruptcy and the family sold their house.

The next witness was Dr. Joseph Klein. I thought that Dr. Klein, the independent medical examiner for Commercial Bankers, would be the key to Justin's case. I had to prove that Commercial Bankers "misinterpreted" Dr. Klein's report deliberately in order to justify its refusal to pay Joe's car payments. I wanted to show that Dr. Klein's medical report was, through no fault of his own, incomplete.

Dr. Klein had been asked to conduct his examination in a vacuum. He received no medical history and no job description. He thought he was to determine whether Joe could perform any kind of work *at all.* Dr. Klein's report to Commercial Bankers was therefore ambiguous. The doctor did find that Joe had serious back problems and recommended that he wear a special support corset, have physical therapy, and be placed in cervical and pelvic traction.

As Dr. Klein was testifying, I explained Joe's job to him. I asked the doctor what he thought about Joe's loading and unloading huge reels of cable in his disabled condition.

Klein: "I think, under the circumstances, I don't believe I
         would recommend that he do that sort of activity."
Shernoff: "Would you, medically speaking, say Mr. Ingram
         was disabled from doing that sort of work?"
Klein: "Yes."

The testimony was a big blow to Commercial Bankers'
case. The bottom-line issue in the case was whether Joe's
disability prevented him from doing his job. The only thing
Commercial Bankers had to justify their refusal to pay Joe's
disability claim was Dr. Klein's report and here he was in
court, blowing them out of the water.

After a few other witnesses were called, the closing arguments began. I don't believe I have ever been as angry in
court as I was when I began this argument.

"I submit to you, ladies and gentlemen, whether
this is good faith and fair dealing. Is this guarding
Joe's rights with trust and fidelity? Is this the way
you'd like your rights guarded with trust and fidelity?

"As soon as Commercial Bankers received Dr.
Klein's report, they sent a letter to Mr. Ingram telling
him that Dr. Klein's report said he could work as a
truck driver. Dr. Klein didn't [say] that, at all. As a
matter of fact, if Commercial Bankers had invested
a dollar for a phone call, Dr. Klein would have told
them exactly what he told you folks.

"The repossession at the post office is incredible. . . . But it goes from bad to worse. Mr. Ingram
writes them a letter and explains. A three-page letter.
Even after the repossession, he is giving them another chance.

"He wrote, 'I have been embarrassed. I have been
humiliated. I'm asking for an eight-year-old boy who

is seriously ill and in dire need of a reliable automobile. . . . [I am] very hard-pressed financially . . .
[I] don't have the funds to repair my old Plymouth
. . . [we] require a reliable automobile . . . your kind
and prompt attention . . .'

"Frankly, I think Mr. Ingram is displaying a lot of
good character. If my car were repossessed or if it
were my child . . . I would never write a letter asking
for kind and prompt attention. My letter would have
some words in there that would make your hair curl."

After I finished, Tim Sargent, the very able lawyer for
Commercial Bankers, tried to calm the atmosphere in the
courtroom. He did a good job. He reviewed practically every
point of the testimony and attempted to identify inconsisten-
cies. He tried to show that Joe may have been responsible for
part of the problem by not cooperating with Commercial
Bankers. He concluded by stating:

"I don't think that the conduct of Commercial
Bankers is any more unreasonable than the conduct
of Mr. Ingram. I think this is what you will find. That
is why you will find a defense verdict."

It took the jury one day to reach the verdict. They awarded
Joe $128,000 in compensatory damages (for mental and
emotional distress) and $872,001 in punitive damages. The
total was $1,000,001. Later on, I asked the jury foreman
why they decided on the odd figure of one dollar over $1
million. The jury, he said, wanted this unusual amount so
Commercial Bankers would remember it. I was elated and
the Ingrams felt vindicated. I thought that justice had been
done.

The Ingrams were very grateful to the Muscular Dystrophy Association for all its help with Justin, and Joe told me he wanted to donate half of the punitive-damage award to the Muscular Dystrophy Association. I thought this was terrific, and I immediately contacted MDA in New York to tell them of Joe's charity. Joe signed an agreement donating "one-half of his net recovery of punitive damages to do the research and development necessary to find a cure or otherwise alleviate the effects of the duchenne-type muscular dystrophy." The donation was to be known as the "Justin Ingram" trust fund.

We were well satisfied until a bomb dropped on us. Commercial Bankers made the usual motion for a new trial. I did not think the motion would be granted because I felt the evidence was strong and that Commercial Bankers deserved severe punishment. The judge felt otherwise. He granted Commercial Bankers' motion unless we agreed to a reduction of the compensatory damages and agreed to eliminate punitive damages altogether. I could not believe it.

The law which permits a judge to grant a new trial or reduce verdicts is complicated. Although there are different viewpoints, generally a trial judge may reduce a jury's verdict if the judge feels—after reweighing all the evidence—that the facts do not support the verdict. Most people do not know about this law. Indeed, it makes little sense to have a full-blown jury trial, to let a jury set an amount, and then have the judge impose his own idea of what the appropriate amount should be. Understandably, a judge should grant a new trial when a prejudicial legal error occurs or where one side does not receive a fair trial. In the case of Justin's car, the judge did not find a legal error. He acknowledged the trial was fair; he simply thought that the evidence did not support the verdict. I disagreed, but there was nothing I could do except file an appeal with the District Court of Appeals.

Appeals take a long time in California, and two or three years is commonplace. This delay was placing a great financial burden on the Ingrams because they were bankrupt and matters were getting worse. After our appeal had been on file for a year, Joe came to me in desperation. He wanted me to make a stab at settling. I was sure the insurance company would not pay for anything near what the verdict had been. After all, Commercial Bankers now had the upper hand. I approached Tim Sargent on the subject, and he was very understanding. After some negotiations he came through with a $100,000 settlement offer. Joe's only choice was to accept it. Since the jury's original award was $128,000 in compensatory damages, the settlement amounted to $28,000 less compensation and zero for punitive damages. Still, $100,000 was a lot of money for Joe and allowed the family to start a new life and get on their feet again.

Because Joe received no money for punitive damages, he could not make Justin's donation to the Muscular Dystrophy Association.

Since *Ingram v. Commercial Bankers,* I have worked hard to change the law that allows a judge to reduce a jury's verdict. I have deep respect for our jury system. I have tried to rationalize the judge's decision by blaming the system that would allow this to occur. The next year I was elected president of the California Trial Lawyers Association (CTLA). I devoted a substantial amount of time attempting to introduce legislation that would cure this defect in the law.

The insurance industry vigorously opposes any change in the law that allows a judge to reduce jury verdicts. That law still remains, but we will keep trying to change it. However, with great effort by many trial lawyers, we were able to convince the legislature to pass a prejudgment-interest law. The law makes it possible, in some cases, to collect interest on damages from the day a lawsuit is filed.

The *Ingram* case was an enlightening experience. It convinced me of the value of our civil jury system and what it means to the average citizen. The jury is truly the cornerstone of our system of justice. We, as a society, should guard constantly against attempts to weaken it for the sake of efficiency or advantage by any one group. The weaker our jury system becomes, the less valuable our individual rights become.

CHAPTER 11

Getting a Piece of the Rock: How a Trucker Won $1 Million

Case Study: *Pistorius v. Prudential*

Uncovering elaborate insurance schemes often requires great effort. Yet, in some cases, the testimony of insurance agents is so deplorable that little digging is necessary. That was the case with Raymond Pistorius, a 42-year-old truck driver who decided to battle Prudential, the largest insurance company in America.

For almost 20 years Ray was a long- and short-haul trucker. One cold day in December, Ray was driving down an icy road in Weed, California, when his truck jackknifed. The truck was totaled and Ray was hospitalized for nine days, suffering chronic pain in his neck, left shoulder, and back. However, 12 days before the accident, at the urging of a Prudential Insurance Company agent, Ray bought a disability policy which promised to pay $300 a month for 15 years if he were disabled.

After the accident, doctors prescribed painkillers, tranquilizers, and rest for several months before allowing Ray to return to work. Despite discomfort, he began driving again two months later. Then, about a year after his accident, Ray slipped while climbing into the truck's cab. That fall aggravated his injuries and intensified the pain. "I couldn't drive anymore," Ray testified at the trial. "If I turned the steering wheel or depressed the clutch, my left side would go dead on me. I'd lose the grip in my left hand and I would just let go."

Several doctors treated Ray and classified him as disabled. He began receiving his monthly benefits from Prudential, and they continued for about two years. Then Prudential decided to terminate Ray's policy because he was attending a vocational school. Ray protested, and, following additional evidence from doctors, Prudential restored his benefits.

Five years later, Prudential apparently became impatient with Ray's slow rehabilitation, although nothing in Ray's policy required him to seek job retraining. In fact, he could have stayed home and vegetated, and the monthly benefits would have been just as payable. Nevertheless, Prudential told Ray that he was no longer totally disabled from any occupation and that his monthly checks would stop. Once again, he protested.

Finally, Ray was so frustrated that he went to Lee Mandel, a Mount Shasta, California, lawyer who wrote a letter to Prudential claims adjuster Jane Garrett, informing her that a lawsuit had been filed. Garrett wrote back saying that benefits would be restored, and included a check for all amounts due. However, Ray's lawsuit had been filed, and eight months later Prudential filed a countersuit to recover all payments made to Ray up to, but not including, the lump-sum payment sent earlier. The trial was set in Yreka, California, the seat of Siskiyou County.

Shortly before the trial, Mandel asked me to take over the case, and I accepted. The trial began as scheduled in Judge James Kleaver's courtroom. Testimony was taken from 11 witnesses, including Ray, four doctors, Ray's neighbor, a man Ray had worked for, a former state rehabilitation officer, an accountant, and two Prudential employees. We wanted to show a persistent, abusive pattern of behavior that was calculated to eliminate Ray's benefits.

On the third day of trial, I called Burdell Benson to the stand as an adverse witness. Benson had worked for Prudential for 25 years. He carried the title of claims consultant. He had the Prudential claim file in his hand as he testified about the decision to terminate payments.

Shernoff: "Now, at this point, did somebody have a question concerning his continuing disability?"

Benson: "Yes, there was a question."

Q. "And did the claims examiner suggest a complete workup?" [A workup is a medical examination.]

A. "He suggested a workup, yes."

Q. "Complete workup, according to the claims file. Did he suggest an interview with the attending physician?"

A. "Yes, he did."

Q. "Was a letter sent to Mr. Pistorius?"

A. "Yes, it was."

Q. "That is approximately six days after the note in the file to have a complete workup and to interview the physician, is that correct?"

A. "Yes."

Q. "In that letter Prudential tells Mr. Pistorius that his benefits are being terminated, is that correct?"

A. "Yes, it does."

Q. "This letter was sent to him without any other workup being done, is that correct?"

A. "Correct."

Q. "There was no interview with the physician, is that correct?"

A. "Correct."
Q. "After that, did Mr. Pistorius write a protest letter?"
A. "Yes, he did."
Q. "After the protest letter, then Prudential commenced the investigation, did it not?"
A. "Yes."
Q. "Had Mr. Pistorius not complained to Prudential, there would have been no investigation, is that correct?"
A. "True."
Q. "And he never would have received any more benefits from that date forward, isn't that correct?"
A. "That's true."

I next focused on the attempt five years later to terminate Ray's benefits. This occurred after a telephone call Prudential made to Ray's treating physician, Dr. Roger Howe. He testified that Ray was disabled and that he told the Prudential agent during the telephone conversation that Ray's condition was unchanged. I questioned Benson about that call.

Shernoff: "The file reflects, does it not, that a Prudential claims adjuster had a telephone conversation with Dr. Howe, is that correct?"
Benson: "Correct."
Q. "Who was the adjuster?"
A. "Frederick Totten."
Q. "Did Dr. Howe tell Frederick Totten that Mr. Pistorius's condition was unchanged?"
A. "Yes."
Q. "Was there any change in what Dr. Howe told Frederick Totten on that date, over his condition for the last four years?"

A. "Telephone report is basically the same, yes."

Q. "The next thing in the file shows a telephone call from Mr. Pistorius, because, as we saw, there was a request that Mr. Pistorius call, is that correct?"

A. "Correct."

Q. "According to the file, what did Mr. Pistorius tell Mr. Totten when he called in, would you read that to the jury?"

A. " 'Mr. Pistorius called me per my request to discuss his claim and was cooperative. [We] pointed out to him that we had allowed benefits for six and a half years and were concerned with when he might be able to resume work. He related that the State Rehabilitation had given him training in the repair of automobile engines and he sought work in this area, but no employer would hire him because he needed a clean bill of health and [the attending physician] could not give it to him.' "

Q. "The next thing that happened, as far as Mr. Pistorius was concerned, six days later, his benefits were terminated, is that right?"

A. "Correct."

Q. "You made that decision, didn't you?"

A. "I was one of those that made it, yes."

Q. "At that point in time, if you had any question about his condition of disability, did you have a right under the policy to have him examined by a physician of your own choosing?"

A. "We did."

Q. "You did not elect to do that at that time, did you?"

A. "No, sir. We did not."

Q. "Did you feel that terminating his benefits at this time was fair to the insured?"

A. "Absolutely."

When he replied, "Absolutely," we had reached a turning point in the trial. I could start to sense the jurors' anger. The jurors were beginning to get the picture. Prudential tried to terminate Ray's benefits once without an investigation. Prudential tried again three years later, until an investigation showed that Ray was still disabled. Then, two years after this, his treating physician told them that Ray's condition was unchanged. The logical, simply inescapable conclusion was that "unchanged" meant he was still disabled. Dr. Howe said Ray could be retrained for a sedentary occupation, but that did not change his disability status.

The jury had already heard Ray testify that, when he was told his benefits would be canceled, he called Prudential immediately and spoke with Frederick Totten in the claims department. Totten told Ray his benefits had been paid for all those years, including a period of retraining, and now they would stop—in effect, he told Ray, "Too bad."

Ray asked Totten why Prudential was doing this when his disability was evident and confirmed by the doctors. He asked Totten to arrange for an independent medical examination if the company didn't believe him. Totten contended that the company was not required to do that. Ray told Totten he was going to contact the State Department of Insurance to report Prudential's behavior, and, according to Ray's testimony, Totten told him, if he did, that Prudential would try to get back the benefits paid for the past six years.

I kept Benson on the stand, building my case.

Shernoff: "In any event, the complaint to the Department of Insurance was received from Prudential and the file reflects that the Department of Insurance asked to see the [Pistorius] file, is that correct?"

Benson: "Yes."

Q. "The file was reviewed with an officer from the

Department of Insurance, and a report was in the file, was it not?"

A. "It was."

Q. "In this inspection report, is it true that the Department of Insurance directed Prudential to have an independent medical examination by a physician of their own choosing and to send a copy of the examination report to the Department of Insurance?"

A. "He suggested that we get an examination and that he receive a copy of it."

Q. "Following that request, Prudential set up an independent medical exam, did it not?"

A. "We do try to cooperate with the commissioner whenever we can, and we did order the exam."

I knew that Prudential had not been content just to arrange the examination and let things happen. Prudential actually told the doctor chosen to do the examination that Ray's own physician had not certified his disability and that Ray had been retrained to repair small engines and motors. As the testimony unfolded, it became obvious that both assertions were untrue.

Shernoff: "Now let's get to the special instructions to the doctor."

Benson: [Reading] " 'We are referring Mr. Pistorius for an independent medical examination to determine if he is totally disabled, unable to perform every occupation for which he is reasonably fitted by education, training, or experience. It should be noted that Mr. Pistorius's physician has not certified to his disability. And Mr. Pistorius has been retrained in the repair of small engines and motors.' "

Q. "And this instruction was to be given to Dr. Howland, who was selected as the independent medical examiner?"

A. "Yes."

Q. "The reference there that Mr. Pistorius's physician
had not certified to his disability is totally false,
isn't it, sir?"

A. "No, sir."

Q. "Treating physician is Dr. Howe, isn't it?"

A. "Yes."

Q. "Dr. Howe's certification of disability is in the file,
is it not?"

A. "It is over a year old at this point in time."

By this testimony, Benson virtually conceded that Dr.
Howe had certified Ray as disabled. Benson tried to retrieve
the situation for Prudential so he came up with the idea that
the doctor hadn't seen Ray for a year. But this wasn't true at
all. Indeed, Ray had been examined by Dr. Howe much more
recently, and Dr. Howe had communicated this to Prudential
by telephone. This became obvious from the records.

We turned our attention to Dr. Howland's report, in response to the Department of Insurance's requirement, to
Prudential. Prudential had attempted to turn that report to its
advantage. This testimony turned out to include one of the
company's biggest and most embarrassing blunders.

Shernoff: "Dr. Howland sent a report of his examination to
Prudential, did he not?"

Benson: "He did."

Q. "Can you read this report to the jury?"

A. [Reading] " 'As to disability, at this time because
of this painful lesion I would say that since this
man is trained for auto mechanics, I would feel he

could not do anything dealing in auto mechanics. He is trained by experience to be a truck driver, but I would not feel he is satisfactory for truck driving. He is apparently wanting to be a bus driver and indeed he could be a bus driver for two to three hours a day. However, this would imply [that he] simply do the mechanics of driving and would not be available for any emergencies, changing of bus tires, or such things which may or may not come up during the course of driving a bus.' "

Q. "Based upon that report did you feel he was qualified for a job as a school bus driver?"

A. "I did."

Q. "Even though the doctor was saying that he could not do any emergency work and could only work for a couple [of] hours a day?"

A. "Says 'two to three hours a day,' yes."

Q. "But you feel he would be satisfactory for driving a bus with children on it, is that right?"

A. "That is what the doctor told us."

This answer seemed incredible to me. School bus driving was a hazardous chore in Yreka, with its treacherous, winding mountain roads. Dr. Howland had said very clearly in his medical report that Ray might be able to drive a bus two or three hours a day, but that he was definitely not fit for any emergencies, tire changing, that sort of thing. He also suggested that because of the numbness in Ray's neck and arms, he might not be able to drive any large vehicle safely. Benson had instantly transformed from someone who was willing to deprive a disabled person of a meager income into someone who would put the lives of schoolchildren in jeopardy.

I continued:

Shernoff: "When this medical report came in, it was reviewed by another [Prudential] claims examiner, was it not?"

Benson: "Yes."

Q. "Jane Garrett?"

A. "Yes."

Q. "Ms. Garrett looked at the medical report and concluded there was little alternative but to pay the benefits, isn't that right?"

A. "That's what she said."

Q. "You overruled her, didn't you?"

A. "Yes, I did."

Q. "And you overruled her without checking with the doctor for further clarification, isn't that right?"

A. "I overruled her on the basis of the reports in the file."

Q. "My question was, before you overruled her, did you check with the doctor?"

A. "No, sir, I did not check with the doctor."

Q. "That's your own doctor, Dr. Howland, right?"

A. "Yes."

Q. "So after you overruled Ms. Garrett, a letter was sent that it was the opinion of the doctor who performed the independent medical examination that he was no longer disabled and that benefits would not be resumed, is that right?"

A. "We did say it was the opinion of the physician who performed the independent medical exam that he could perform occupational duties."

Q. "Who did you have write that letter?"

A. "Jane Garrett."

Q. "Let me ask you this, Mr. Benson: Do you feel this claim was handled fairly by Prudential Insurance Company?"

A. "Yes, I do."

Q. "You realize that the law requires you to handle claims in good faith?"

A. "Absolutely."

Q. "You realize that the insured depends on you to protect his interests?"

A. "Yes."

Q. "Do you feel you protected Mr. Pistorius's interest in this claim?"

A. "I think we did."

Shernoff: "Your Honor, I have nothing further of this witness."

Under cross-examination, the testimony of Fred Totten, a claims adjuster for Prudential, was equally damaging. The questioning began with Prudential's lawyer, John Lynch.

Lynch: "Did you ever tell Mr. Pistorius that if he went to the Department of Insurance that Prudential would seek recovery of everything that had been paid to him?"

Totten: "Definitely not."

Q. "Did you say anything like that?"

A. "No, I did not."

Q. "Upon what do you base that?"

A. "My recollection of the particular case and the fact that I have never told anyone that if they went to the insurance commissioner we'd attempt to take away or recover any benefits that we have already paid."

Q. "Is there anything in [your notes] to indicate the nature of the conversation you had with Mr. Pistorius at that time?"

A. "By nature, it says that he was cooperative, if that's what you mean by nature."

Q. "Did you mention to him at all at that time that his benefits were to be terminated?"

A. "No, no decision had been made at that time."

Q. "Were you the one that made the decision?"

A. "No, I was not."

Q. "Did you ever have any other telephone calls from Mr. Pistorius?"

A. "Not to my recollection."

Lynch: "That's all I have, thank you."

Totten's testimony was in direct opposition to what Ray had said from the witness stand about Prudential's threats to "recover" back benefits. Indeed, Prudential was countersuing for back benefits.

I remembered that Totten had used the word "recover" when he wrote an office memorandum after his telephone conversation with Ray and was sure he had forgotten. I asked him to explain what "recover" means in Prudential parlance.

Shernoff: "You say that you would never tell anybody that you [would] attempt to recover benefits?"

Totten: "I never told any insured that."

Q. "What does the term 'recover' benefits mean?"

A. "It means to take back what was once paid out."

Q. "Now, there is a difference between terminating benefits and recovering benefits, isn't there?"

A. "Yes, there is."

Q. "Terminating means that you're just going to stop the benefits. And recovering means to go back and take what has already been paid, right?"

A. "Yes."

Q. "Now, after this phone conversation [with Mr. Pistorius], there are some internal memos in the file, isn't that correct?"

A. "Yes, there are."

Q. "That last sentence of one memo says, 'I suggest we recover and leave door open if he wishes to contest our action.' Doesn't it say that?"

A. "Yes, it does."

Q. "It uses the term 'recover,' does it not?"

A. "Yes, it does."

Q. "That means go back and get the back payments, doesn't it?"

A. "No, it does not."

Q. "Isn't that what you just told the jury it meant?"

A. "No."

Q. "Well, you just told the court and jury in response to my question that the word 'recover' means to go back and get the back payments and the word 'terminate' means to stop the payments. Didn't you testify to that, sir?"

A. "Yes, I did."

Q. "And the Prudential claims file, right after the conversation, says 'recover,' doesn't it?"

A. "Yes, it does."

Q. "It doesn't say 'terminate,' does it? It says 'recover.' "

A. "Yes, it does."

Q. "That means to go back and get the back payments, doesn't it?"

Totten: "No, it does not."

The jury looked at Totten in bewilderment. As I had done with Benson, I asked Totten how he felt about the Prudential way of doing business.

Shernoff: "In reviewing the file, as a Prudential Insurance examiner, are you proud of the way Prudential handled this claim?"

Totten: "I think it was handled fairly. I think it was han-
   dled competently and professionally."
   Q. "Is this the type of fairness that you extend to all
   of your insureds?"
   A. "Yes, it is."
Shernoff: "Thank you."

Now it was time to show the jury Prudential's wealth. As
the largest American insurance company, it has assets that
are astounding. We put accountant Michael S. Pavlik, a
Yreka resident, on the stand.

The testimony by Pavlik revealed that, for the year in
question, the insurance company had total assets of $50
billion, liabilities of $48 billion, and a surplus (net worth) of
$2 billion. From this came $1.3 billion paid out in dividends
and $360 million paid in taxes, leaving a net income of
roughly $270 million.

When it came time to cross-examine the accountant, Prudential's counsel, Lynch, had a tough job on his hands. There
was no way he could minimize Prudential's tremendous
wealth. And he wanted to get him off the stand quickly. He
wisely asked Pavlik only a few questions about what would
happen to the company's surplus if Prudential dissolved, and
dismissed him.

My summation to the jury began early the next day. I
reviewed the testimony in near-chronological order, pointing
out Prudential's outrageous conduct by acting first, investigating afterward, and ignoring the investigation if it didn't
suit them, in order to save some $30,000. I cited statistics
from trial exhibits that doctors had certified Ray's total disability and that his attempts to retrain himself should not be
held against him.

I recounted key episodes.

"Now . . . they make a phone call to Dr. Howe.
You recall Dr. Howe, the doctor from Mount Shasta.
Very honest doctor, credible doctor, family physician, wants to help people, wants to treat people.
Prudential calls him and there is the record of it right
in their own claim file. Dr. Howe tells Mr. Totten,
'Ray will be in today.' There was a phone call on [the
same day]. Prudential left a message with the doctor's office: 'When Mr. Pistorius comes in, have him
call us.'

"Their next note in the claim file is [the next day].
This is the picture: the adjuster calls the doctor and
the doctor says, 'He'll be in today later on, I'll examine him. Why don't you call back tomorrow? I'll
have the complete story for you.' The guy comes in,
the adjuster calls back the next day, and Dr. Howe
tells him: 'Ray is still disabled.' Perhaps in the future
he could do some sedentary job with retraining. But
no employer would hire him for any occupation re-
quiring physical labor. It's not only in Prudential's
own claim file, it's in the doctor's record.

"Can you believe it? Right after they hang up the
phone, on the same day, they tell Mr. Pistorius: 'We
just talked to Dr. Howe and he says you are not
disabled, and we're cutting you off.' Mr. Pistorius
tells them that his training hasn't been successful,
that no doctor would give him a clean bill of health,
et cetera, et cetera. Then Mr. Pistorius says, 'Well,
wait a second, at least give me the benefit of the
doubt. Pick a doctor of your own choosing. You've
got a right under the policy to do it.' Mr. Pistorius
says: 'Don't believe Dr. Howe; don't believe all the
doctors; don't believe Social Security; don't believe
anybody—get your own doctor.' They say, 'Oh, we

don't have to examine you.' And then when he finally
says, 'I'm going to file a complaint with the Department of Insurance,' they tell him, 'You do that and
we'll sue you for all the back benefits.' "

The company's arrogance made me especially angry.

"Do they have the courage and the decency to
come into this courtroom and say, 'That's bad, that
was a mistake. We're a proud company. We shouldn't
really be doing things like that.' No. They take the
oath and they say, 'That's fair. That's the way we
handle claims.' I wouldn't have believed it unless I
heard it."

Finally, I talked about damages. I explained that Ray was
entitled to the cash value of his policy: $17,200. I also
pointed out that Ray had suffered so much humiliation and
anger that an old ulcer started acting up. Ray had been
hospitalized for fear he was having a heart attack. I recounted
Ray's financial woes, explaining how he had had to borrow
money and that his credit cards had been canceled. Translat-
ing Ray's mental distress into money was difficult.

"It's a subjective thing. The law doesn't give any
fixed standard or guidance or formula. I think if I had
to give you some guidance, I'd figure somewhere
between $10,000 and $50,000. Some of you might
think higher, some of you might think lower. Nobody
can argue with it, really."

It was the punitive damages issue, though, that allowed me
to say what I really wanted to. I explained to the jury that the
law says that deterrence and punishment have little effect if
the wealth of the defendant allows it to absorb the amount of

the damages with no discomfort. I wanted the jury to make the award a little bit uncomfortable for Prudential.

I pleaded with the jury to take a good look at the evidence, specifically the company's annual report as it was explained by the accountant.

> "After they pay all their expenses; after they pay all their dividends; after they've reserved for all claims; even after they pay their income taxes, their net income is $270 million per year, or approximately $5 million per week, or approximately a million dollars for every working day. That's profit. That is what is left after they pay all their expenses. A million dollars a working day."

I pointed out that a court would certainly not hesitate to fine a few days' pay if an individual had swindled $30,000. Or what about the company surplus—a surplus of over $2 billion? A court would find nothing wrong with fining an ordinary individual criminal 1 percent of his surplus.

Then, after I had explained the figures and repeated my philosophy of punishment and deterrence, I ended my summation in my customary tone.

> "I think I have really talked long enough. I think I have done my job. That's all I can do. I can subpoena the records. I can bring them into this courtroom. I can put Prudential on the witness stand. I can expose everything. I can let you see it. I can let you feel it. And my job is done. In a few minutes it's going to be your job. You are going to have to talk to that company. You are going to have to speak for Mr. Pistorius and for all the people, because punitive damages involve society. You are going to be talking with this verdict."

Lynch's argument was a painstaking recitation of medical details and other irrelevant information. The case was then turned over to the jury. After about six hours of deliberation, they came in with an astounding verdict. Ray was awarded compensatory damages for his mental distress of $45,000. Then the jury socked Prudential with a $1 million punitive damage award. It was the largest punitive award ever assessed against Prudential on behalf of a policyholder.

Judge Kleaver rejected Prudential's motion for a new trial. Prudential appealed, claiming that the amount of the award was excessive. Even the Court of Appeals upheld the $1 million award and concentrated, just like the jury, on Prudential's misrepresentations of facts and on the company's courtroom concession that it was standard procedure to cut off disability payments and not reinstate them unless the policyholder complained. In an opinion notable for its simplicity, the three appellate judges concluded that there was:

> "no doubt concerning the existence of substantial evidence of emotional distress, consisting of anger, anxiety, humiliation, and frustration, due to actions of defendant."

The court also concluded that Prudential acted, at the very least, with a conscious disregard of Pistorius's rights and he was therefore entitled to punitive damages. As for the punitive damages, the judges justified the amount and wrote:

> "For the year [in question], defendant's net income after taxes and dividends was $270 million. Its gross assets were in excess of $50 billion and its net worth $2 billion. The award of $1 million was thus .00002 percent of its gross assets. And it was approximately one-twentieth of one percent of its net worth."

Summing up the presentation of facts in the case, the judges made note of numerous misrepresentations and irregularities and then wrote:

"Defendant repeatedly testified its handling of the claim was proper and in accordance with its standard operating procedures, it handled this claim fairly, it handled all its claims in the same fashion as it handled this one, and it would handle plaintiff's claim the same way if it had to do it all over again."

Prudential's petition to the California Supreme Court was denied and the case was over. Shortly thereafter, Prudential paid the full amount plus interest. Ray Pistorius truly did get a piece of the rock.

CHAPTER 12

Life Insurance: A Widow Takes On a Giant

Case Study: *Frazier v. Metropolitan Life*

In life insurance, there should be little room for argument. In disability insurance, an argument may arise over whether a person is disabled; fire insurance companies may dispute the amount of damage; medical insurers may argue over what is covered and what is not. With life insurance, once the company is presented with the death certificate, it should pay.

But life insurance companies have found a way to complicate matters. Many life policies have double-indemnity provisions: this means the beneficiary will be paid double if the policyholder meets with an accidental death. Often a controversy develops over the definition of accidental death, and these controversies expose life insurance to the world of bad faith.

Mary Frazier v. Metropolitan Life Insurance Company was a bad faith case if ever I saw one. The amount of the double-indemnity provision was $12,000.

Mary's battle with Metropolitan began after her 23-year-old husband drowned. David and Mary had been happily married for five years, and they had one child. His postal service employee benefits included a $12,000 double-indemnity life insurance policy. According to the policy, the widow expected $24,000.

David, his brother, Curtis, and their mother, Mae, liked to go fishing near the Channel Islands, about 75 miles up the coast from Los Angeles. One day Mae talked her two sons into accompanying her on a trip out to the islands on the *Electra*, a fishing vessel she liked and had been on before. The *Electra* left the harbor at night and by morning was in place for fishing.

Sixty passengers were on board, and most fished the entire day before the *Electra* headed back to the harbor in the early evening. As the boat entered Channel Island Harbor in Ventura County, David was walking near the outside rail. Suddenly he was in the water. Mae, who was in the boat's cabin, said she saw him fall over backward into the water. Crew members claimed that David screamed, "Don't let them get me!" and jumped overboard.

There was some confusion about what happened after he hit the water. Some crew members claimed that he resisted rescue by swimming away from the boat. Mae Frazier remembered clearly that she had shouted to David, screaming to him to swim away from the boat toward the rocks, about 75 feet away. No one disputed that David was treading water for a while before he disappeared beneath the surface and drowned.

Metropolitan paid Mary Frazier the first $12,000 of the death benefit and then refused to pay the double-indemnity payment of $12,000. A claims representative wrote Mary and told her that the company had made a thorough investigation of the events and concluded that David had committed suicide.

This was news to his widow because Mary knew that her husband was not suicidal. She told Metropolitan that she and David were regular churchgoers, and suicide was contrary to their religion. Indeed, Mary was so disturbed by the allegations of suicide and so embarrassed that she felt compelled to leave Los Angeles and find refuge with relatives in Kansas. When she returned five months later, she decided that the stigma of suicide was too great to bear and that the family name had to be cleared. She engaged the services of attorney Hal B. Williams, Jr., one of Los Angeles' finest personal injury lawyers.

Williams brought a suit against the owners of the *Electra*. He claimed that debris on the deck may have caused David's fall into the sea and that the crew failed to use proper man-overboard and rescue procedures. A Ventura County Superior Court found the boat crew had been negligent and their negligence caused David's death. They awarded Mary damages for David's death.

The second lawsuit, the bad faith case against Metropolitan, was filed later, but did not come to trial until four years after Mary had won her negligence case. I was now on the case, and the issues were clear to us. I was really confident about the suit because we had such strong evidence. Two key documents—one an internal Metropolitan memo and the other a letter sent by the insurance company to its investigators—would give the jury a textbook definition of bad faith.

The internal memo was written by Claims Supervisor Charles Pfaffenbach, who died before the case came to trial. He would not be able to explain the memo dated *one day before* Mary Frazier was informed by Metropolitan that, because of the company's suicide finding, she was not eligible for the $12,000 accidental-death benefit.

Pfaffenbach wrote the memo to his boss, Albert Danz, assistant manager in charge of claims. It said:

> "I still doubt we could sustain a denial in court. Unless you want to deny now [and] try for a compromise later when she complains."

That memo meant one thing: Pfaffenbach had reviewed all the evidence, decided the claim was payable, and admitted that any denial would not hold up in court. The memo was dynamite—and I knew what I could do with it in front of a jury.

Danz's written response was:

"Deny, refer any protests [to me]."

I knew when I first saw this memo that it would be the focus of the trial. No matter what Metropolitan tried to do, or how hard the company lawyers tried to divert the jurors' attention from the memo, those handwritten words would demonstrate Metropolitan's bad faith.

A letter from Metropolitan to Retail Credit, an investigating firm that worked closely with insurance companies, was one more nail in the coffin. The concluding sentence read:

"As it would appear that the insured attempted suicide, we would appreciate a full report of investigation concerning any motive for suicide."

It then seemed to me that Metropolitan was actually asking Retail Credit *to find* motives for *suicide.* Period. The end.

The trial began in the Los Angeles County Superior Court, with the Honorable M. Ross Bigelow presiding. Hal Williams represented Mary Frazier. He had asked me to join him as our combined experience—his thorough knowledge of the case and my bad faith practice—made a strong team.

Metropolitan was defended by Adams, Duque & Hazeltine, a Los Angeles firm that had represented many insurance companies in bad faith actions. James Willcox was their team leader.

I had hoped that we would be able to use the results of the earlier negligence lawsuit against the *Electra* owners to show that a jury had already decided that David's death was accidental. However, Judge Bigelow ruled that, since Metropolitan had not been a part of the earlier lawsuit, nothing from that case could be brought into this trial because suicide had not been an issue in the negligence suit.

In another ruling, the judge decided he wanted Metropolitan's liability established before the jury determined appropriate damage amounts. He split the trial in two: bifurcating, in legal parlance. The cause of death, the insurance company's liability, and the extent of the liability would be determined first. Following jury decisions on those issues, appropriate amounts for mental and emotional distress and punitive damages would be decided.

The questions that had to be answered during the first phase of the trial were:

1: Did David Frazier's death result from accidental means?
2: Did Metropolitan violate its duty of good faith and fair dealing in investigating and then denying the claim?
3: Did Metropolitan's conduct amount to malice, oppression, or fraud?

We contended that Metropolitan had no evidence to support suicide. Whatever the conflicting testimony was—from David's relatives on the boat, from members of the crew, or from other passengers—the bottom line was that David had no cause to commit suicide. He had never indicated he was suicidal and had never behaved in an aberrant way—I was certain of this. I was just as certain that Metropolitan had violated its duty of good faith, but those legal issues were more complex.

Metropolitan's major witness on the bad faith issue was

Albert Danz, a nice, grandfatherly man who made a good impression on the stand. Since the time he wrote his note, he had retired from Metropolitan. He was knowledgeable and cooperative as Willcox, the Metropolitan attorney, led him through the Frazier file step by step. It was becoming obvious that Metropolitan's strategy was to have Danz explain away the company's handling of the case.

Danz said it was Pfaffenbach who had doubts about the cause of David's death. On the witness stand, Danz said he reviewed the file independently and made the final decision to deny the claim. In other words, the memo was not indicative of Danz's state of mind, but only of the late Pfaffenbach's, whose state of mind was now out of the reach of mortal man. I had a hunch that Danz's story would fall apart if I cross-examined him properly. He appeared to be an honest man, and I believed he would give honest responses to straightforward questions.

I started by calling his attention to the letter his company had written to Retail Credit to commence the investigation. I was certain that Danz hadn't looked carefully at this letter and was unaware of its significance.

Shernoff: "Before Metropolitan Life Insurance had Retail Credit do any investigation whatsoever, didn't Metropolitan Life Insurance already conclude that this death was apparently due to suicide?"

Danz: "I would say no."

I then asked Danz to turn to the letter to Retail Credit asking them to make an investigation.

Shernoff: "Now, directing your attention to the last paragraph of your letter—Metropolitan's letter to

Retail Credit—isn't it true in fact—in the last paragraph, it says, 'It would appear that the insured attempted suicide. We would appreciate a full report of investigation concerning any motive for suicide'?"

Danz: "Oh, yes."

Q. "Isn't it true, now that you have reviewed the letter, even before any investigation was done that Metropolitan informed Retail Credit that Metropolitan felt that this was probably a suicide and that they should get the motives for suicide?"

A. "Well, it does state, 'It would appear,' and 'We would appreciate a full report of investigation concerning any motive for suicide,' et cetera."

Q. "Let me ask you this: If you're going to ask somebody to do an investigation for you, don't you want to have a full and fair investigation?"

A. "Yes, sir."

Q. "At the time that you asked for this investigation, isn't it true that the people at Metropolitan didn't know one way or another . . . whether this was an accident or a suicide?"

A. "Well—to tell you—it does appear that—it is not definite, one way or the other."

Q. "Do you see that last paragraph there?"

A. "Yes, sir."

Q. "The date that this letter was written is before any investigation took place; isn't that correct?"

A. "Yes, sir. This was ordering an investigation."

Q. "Okay. So before any investigation took place, the claims department and Metropolitan had already formed the opinion that this appeared to be suicide—right?"

A. "Well—I guess it could be considered that."
Q. "That's what the letter states; doesn't it?"
Danz: "Yes."

This was the breakthrough I had been looking for. Danz started out stating that there was no premature conclusion of suicide, but then he had to agree reluctantly that, before any outside investigation was requested, the claims department at Metropolitan had decided the death was a suicide.

There was some conflict among witnesses about what happened after Retail Credit's investigative reports came back to Metropolitan. At first this looked as if Metropolitan wanted to be more thorough before making up its mind. On closer examination, it appeared that the additional information being sought was merely corroborative evidence to substantiate the claim denial. For example, Metropolitan was relying upon one story which had David Frazier hallucinating in Vietnam War flashbacks. We knew this was incorrect because David's army time was spent in Hawaii. He never set foot in Vietnam.

Danz was getting tired on the witness stand. I could see that Willcox, the Metropolitan attorney, was upset. Besides the Adams, Duque & Hazeltine lawyers, the insurance company had several people from its legal department in the courtroom to observe the proceedings. They looked generally unhappy and downcast as Danz continued to testify.

I had the handwritten document blown up on a three-foot-by-five-foot cardboard display board. There was no mistaking what it said. I approached Danz gently. First I read the memo out loud:

"We now have additional reports which only confirm what we already know. While there is considerable opinion that he did commit suicide, I still doubt we could sustain a denial in court."

Then I asked:

Shernoff: "Did you see that?"
Danz: "Yes, sir."
Q. "Who was Mr. Pfaffenbach writing that to?"
A. "Me, sir."
Q. "When he said, 'I still doubt we could sustain a denial in court,' in your mind what was he referring to by the word 'court'?"
A. "I would imagine a court of law."
Q. "Did you at this time ask him why he had those doubts?"
A. "No, sir, I don't recall asking him."
Q. "When he wrote on the bottom of that, 'unless you want to deny now, try for a compromise later when she complains'; do you see that?"
A. "Yes, sir."
Q. "Would it be true, sir, then, that if she'd never complained at all, she would not ever be in a position to get a compromise?"
A. "Well, I will take it if there was no comeback, that she was satisfied with the situation."
Q. "If there was no comeback, the widow would be satisfied with the decision and there would be no compromise payment—is that right?"
A. "Yes, sir."
Q. "That would be the end of the matter?"
A. "Yes, sir."
Q. "Now, when you got that memo from Mr. Pfaffenbach, you just wrote on here—these are your words, 'Deny, refer any protests [to me].' "
A. "Yes."
Q. "Between the time you got the memo from Mr. Pfaffenbach and when you wrote the words 'Deny,

> refer any protests [to me],' did you do anything
> other than review the file?' "
> A. "No, sir."
> Q. "Did you talk to anybody?"
> Danz: "No, sir, not that I recall."

This was all the ammunition I needed to make my closing argument. I was sure that I had proved beyond a shadow of a doubt that Metropolitan knew the claim was payable but had tried to wriggle out of it.

In my closing argument for this phase of the trial, I had to convince the jury that the death was an accident, not suicide—and that Metropolitan's handling of the claim was in bad faith. Rather than concentrating on the evidence we brought to court, I decided to use the evidence that came right from Metropolitan's own witness and its own documents. I first reminded the jury about Danz's testimony concerning Metropolitan's version of the facts.

> "Let me read you the question I asked [Mr. Danz]
> and the answer he gave: Their version of the facts. I
> asked him, 'Assuming it was true David Frazier said
> "Don't let them get me. Don't let them get me." Then
> assume he put a hand on the safety rail, and jumped
> overboard.' "
> "I said to Danz, 'Those facts, sir, would not indi-
> cate that somebody is trying to destroy himself,
> would it?'
> "And his answer was—Mr. Danz's answer under
> oath—'I have to go along with that.'
> "So either way, either version—he accidentally
> fell overboard or he suffered delusions and jumped—
> supports [death by] accidental means under the defi-
> nition of this insurance policy and under the law. I

think Metropolitan knew that, and I'll get into that when I get to their memos.

"He didn't jump overboard and say, 'I want to drown.' There was no suicide note. He was happy. He and Mary had just bought a car the week before. He was married, had a child. No drugs. No alcohol. Pretty good solid citizen for a kid. Worked at a good job, post office. Nothing to support suicide. He went fishing with his family. If he wanted to commit suicide, why wouldn't he do it while they were 50 miles out to sea at night? Do you wait until you get back to the harbor? There just was absolutely nothing to support suicide."

I next reminded the jury of Danz's testimony concerning the letter to the outside investigating firm, Retail Credit. This would give the jury a perspective of Metropolitan's state of mind right from the start.

"This letter was written before they did any investigation whatsoever. All they had in front of them is what Mary Frazier sent them. And now they were going to ask Retail Credit, an investigating agency, to go out and investigate, and in that letter they said, at the bottom, 'As it would appear the insured attempted suicide, we would appreciate a full report of investigation concerning any motive for suicide,' et cetera.

"This is not like an independent investigation where you say to somebody, 'Hey, go out and get all the facts so we can make an intelligent decision.' No, they don't tell them that.

"They tell them: 'We think it's suicide. You go out and get us the motive so we can deny this claim.' And that's exactly what happened from day one. I'll show you exactly how it falls into place.

"When I asked Mr. Danz a question about this letter, I said, 'Okay. So before any investigation took place, the claims department and Metropolitan already formed the opinion that this appeared to be suicide, right?' "

"A. 'Well—I guess—it could be considered that.' "

"Q. 'That's what the letter states, doesn't it?' "

"A. 'Yes.' "

"This is Mr. Danz, their main witness, the guy that denied the claim—under oath—saying before any investigation took place, they already formed the opinion it was suicide.

"Is that conscious disregard of a person's rights? It sure is. Making up your mind before you even have an investigation? It sure is.

"And then directing the investigation to try and come in the way you preconceived it. Is that fair? Is that good faith and fair dealing? That's probably the highest form of conscious disregard of a person's rights under the insurance policy one could imagine."

I did not know what I was going to say about the crucial memos until I got to that point in my argument. Somehow I always have great faith that a jury will know that I really believe what I am saying when it comes from the heart.

"Ladies and gentlemen, I think that memo speaks more loudly than anything else in this case. It says what they had on their mind, what they did, and why they did it. It certainly says more than what Mr. Willcox is going to try to tell you three or four or five or six or seven years later. That is the proof of the pudding right there.

"We were able to get their in-house memos through court process, and they tell the story. Metropolitan knew they didn't have enough reason to deny this claim. They knew they should have paid this claim, but, instead of doing the fair and right thing, they tried to deny it and hoped to get away perhaps by paying nothing at all if there was no complaint. And if the poor lady complained, 'try for a compromise.'

"Now, if that's the way to do insurance business in this country, God help us on our insurance claims. This is conscious disregard of a person's rights in the highest form, and luckily we have their own memos to prove it.

"Just put that memo against the letter that they sent out when they denied the claim. Here is what is going on at One Madison Avenue. Here is what is going on behind closed doors. Here is what the real thoughts are, and here is what goes to Mary Frazier, in L.A., a letter that says, in fact, 'We have made a most thorough investigation in this matter.' They made an investigation in this matter directed only towards proving their preconceived notion that there was a suicide and that's it.

"They tell Mary Frazier that [investigation shows] under the circumstances death was due to self-destruction. That's what they tell her, but they say in their own memos, 'We don't have enough to sustain a denial in court.'

"Ladies and gentlemen, I think you know what this case is about. It's about whether an insurance company treated a claimant fairly in good faith or was guilty of conscious disregard of her rights."

The jury came back with the following special findings: they found the death accidental, they found Metropolitan's claims handling was in bad faith, and they found that Metropolitan's claims handling amounted to malice. The malice finding was important because it would allow us to put in evidence of Metropolitan's financial worth and to argue for punitive damages.

The second phase of the trial went quickly. We put Mary Frazier on the witness stand to testify about the mental distress she suffered when Metropolitan told her that her husband killed himself and how her emotions turned to anger.

We then put into evidence Metropolitan's financial report. We showed that Metropolitan's income at the time was $371 million, or just slightly over $1 million per day. This was after all expenses, dividends, and taxes were paid. We also put into evidence that Metropolitan's net worth (they call it surplus) was $2,354,000,000.

What would a responsible punishment be? I asked the jury to punish Metropolitan Life approximately one or two weeks' worth of earnings. This was somewhere between $7 million and $12 million.

Metropolitan's lawyer, James Willcox, made an argument which, in essence, claimed that being caught was punishment enough. He put it this way:

> "You are not required to have a finding of punitive damages, and I ask you to consider and think to yourself—I don't know how recently any of you have been stopped by a policeman or even gotten a parking ticket, but something where you've been fined. Sure, it hurts to pay the fine. It also hurts just to get the ticket. Not just to be caught, but to be found to have done something wrong for which you are subject to a fine, to punishment. Even failing to return an overdue library book. I think we all get mad at ourselves.

"Now, counsel has made a very big deal out of the numbers. I told you in opening statement on this aspect of the case that the numbers are going to be big, because Metropolitan is a very large company. They've been doing business for a long, long time, longer than any of us have been alive, and it's grown.

"Look at the actual figures. Look at the actual figures. What would be fair, if in fact you decided any punishment is merited whatsoever. What is an appropriate fine if you were the judge here and saying that this defendant ought to be fined?

"It isn't enough that they've been brought into court and gone through a proceeding and been told that they acted wrongfully, been told that they acted with malice and have been assessed and ordered to pay compensatory damages to the plaintiff. You are the judges saying, 'No, that's not enough. We have to fine this defendant because what has already happened isn't enough.' That's what you have to consider."

The last words in the closing argument were my rebuttal. I just could not stand still for Willcox's argument that Metropolitan should come out of the case with little or no punitive damages.

"Ladies and gentlemen, I'm going to be fairly short in this part, but what I hear Mr. Willcox saying is: 'It's okay. We are in a court of law. We were found guilty of bad faith and malice. Don't punish us.'

"There has to be meaning to the law. To find malice but find no punishment, [no] bad faith, no punishment, is a joke. There is no meaning to the finding.

"The law has to have significance. The law has to
live. The law lives through people like you.

"Let's respect the law. Let's give meaning to the
law. Let's not say, 'We find malice and go on your
way, Metropolitan.' The law should have the same
meaning for everybody, rich or poor. Rich and poor
should be treated alike."

The jury retired for deliberation the following Friday
morning at 9:40 A.M., and continued most of the day. Their
deliberations were broken by a weekend recess and were
resumed Monday morning. After lunch there was a gathering
of lawyers, witnesses, and observers outside the courtroom.
At about 1:30 P.M., we all saw Judge Bigelow slip into the
judge's entrance of the courtroom, and a few minutes later we
were called. The jury had a verdict.

"Ladies and gentlemen of the jury," Judge Bigelow began,
"have you arrived at a verdict?"

"Yes, Your Honor," the foreman responded.

It took a moment or two to get past the technicalities. We
were all waiting for the amounts of damages. The foreman
then said, matter-of-factly:

"Accidental death benefit: $12,000
Emotional distress: $150,000
Punitive damages: $8,000,000"

This was the largest punitive-damage award I had ever
heard a jury come back with in a double-indemnity insurance
bad faith case. A widow, a poor black woman from Watts,
had toppled one of America's corporate giants with an $8
million punishment over a $12,000 claim. I believe it was
justified, and I hope it will convince insurance companies
that they'd better shape up or suffer similar consequences.

When the jury foreman read the amount, most people

thought they hadn't heard correctly. Several reporters appeared magically and the *Los Angeles Times* had a photographer on the scene posthaste. The next day Mary Frazier appeared on the front page of the *Times*. I was standing behind her, and above us the headline read: "Widow Awarded $8 Million." The kicker followed with: "Sued Insurer for Not Paying $12,000 Claim."

When it came time to argue the motion for a new trial, Metropolitan tried to convince the judge that the verdict should not stand at all. Judge Bigelow denied the motion, but reduced the punitive damage award to $2 million.

I thought that Metropolitan should have been happy with that development and would pay. Instead, the company appealed, even after the judge's reduction. The primary point raised in the appeal did not concern the merits of the case but, rather, addressed a technicality: the statute of limitations. This is a law which mandates that lawsuits must be filed within a certain period of time. If the lawsuit is not filed within that period of time, it is lost forever, regardless of how meritorious the case may be. Since the law of "bad faith" is a new legal doctrine, the question of the proper statute of limitations has not yet been resolved firmly. Mary Frazier's lawsuit was filed slightly over two years from the time her claim was denied. She did not realize that she had a lawsuit for quite some time because she accepted the letter she got from Metropolitan, which stated it had made a thorough investigation and had concluded that her husband died by suicide even though she had her own doubts. It was not until the trial of her first lawsuit against the charter boat company that it became obvious that her husband's death was not due to suicide.

The decision of the court of appeals contained good news and bad news. The good news was that it held the jury was justified in finding Metropolitan's conduct to be in bad faith and that the bad faith was clearly established by Metropolitan's own records.

It also found sufficient evidence in the record to support a verdict for damages for emotional distress. The decision held that such damages were not barred by the statute of limitations, which the District Court of Appeals concluded was four years.

Then came the bad news. The District Court of Appeals differentiated between compensatory damages and punitive damages for the purpose of the statute of limitations. It held that the statute of limitations was only two years for the punitive damages. This meant that the punitive damages would be stricken from the judgment and only the damages due under the insurance policy and for emotional distress could be recovered in this case.

This case stands out as one of the best examples of why it may be important to question a denial letter from an insurance company, even if it sounds quite official. In this case, the jury found that what Mary Frazier was told by Metropolitan concerning the death of her husband was not true. The jury found that his death was not due to suicide, but due to accidental means and that the claim should have been paid.

This case shows why it is so important to act as soon as you can if you feel you have suffered damages as a result of some wrongdoing. Sleeping on your rights for too long can be costly.

CHAPTER 13

Some Closing Remarks

If you've followed along with us so far, a number of items should have become clear: That you need never blindly accept an unfavorable insurance company decision if you honestly feel that the denial of your claim was unfair. That you can go a long way toward securing a favorable outcome when filing a claim by doing a minimal amount of "homework" early. Such simple matters of self-help include reading the booklets or other descriptive materials that were supplied with your policy, reviewing the policy itself to be sure you understand fully what is covered or excluded, keeping and updating records diligently, filling out all required forms carefully and thoroughly, and following up on the progress of your claim at the appropriate intervals, as we've discussed earlier.

More important, you should now be aware that there are many steps you can take *on your own* to work toward reversing an initial claim denial. You should also have a clear grasp of your rights as an insured, the obligations of an insurance company to its policyholders, and what the principle of "bad faith" means in the insurance context.

Perhaps most important, you should no longer be intimidated by the possibility that you will have your "day in court" in order to get satisfaction from a reluctant insurer.

196

In the preceding case summaries, we've seen how consumers like you have brought a variety of claims—from as small as a bill for a hearing test to those as significant as lifetime disability payments—to trial, and *have won what they felt was rightfully due them.* Some of these findings have resulted in a second level of awards for punitive damages.

Of course, I am in no way attempting to say that you should rush to trial every time you have a disagreement with your insurance company, any more than I am suggesting that every claim denial is an indicator of "bad faith." What I hope to have done is to provide you with the background, resources, and best steps to take to seek redress *when you sincerely feel that payment has been unfairly withheld from you.*

In the larger perspective, I hope I have underscored the responsibility that you, the consumer, have *to yourself and to society* to challenge apparent instances of "bad faith" practices by any insurance company, no matter its size.

I hope this book will motivate—and assist—*you* to take effective action if and when it becomes necessary.

APPENDIX A

Each state has its own laws and regulations governing all types of insurance. The offices listed in this section are responsible for enforcing these laws as well as providing the public with information about insurance.

Alabama
Alabama Insurance Department
135 South Union Street
Montgomery, AL 36130-3401
(205) 269-3550

Alaska
Alaska Insurance Department
3601 C Street, Suite 740
Anchorage, AK 99503
(907) 562-3626

American Samoa
American Samoa Insurance
   Department
Office of the Governor
Pago Pago, AS 96797
011-684/633-4116

Arizona
Arizona Insurance Department
Consumer Affairs and
   Investigation Division
3030 North Third Street
Phoenix, AZ 85012
(602) 255-4783

Arkansas
Arkansas Insurance Department
Consumer Service Division
400 University Tower Building
12th and University Streets
Little Rock, AR 72204
(501) 371-1813

California
California Insurance Department
Consumer Services Division
3450 Wilshire Boulevard
Los Angeles, CA 90010
1-800-233-9045
Starting January 1991:
300 South Spring Street
Los Angeles, CA 90013

Colorado
Colorado Insurance Division
303 W. Colfax Avenue, 5th Floor
Denver, CO 80204
(303) 620-4300

Connecticut
Connecticut Insurance
    Department
165 Capitol Avenue
State Office Building
Hartford, CT 06106
(203) 297-3800

Delaware
Delaware Insurance Department
841 Silver Lake Boulevard
Dover, DE 19901
(302) 736-4251

District of Columbia
District of Columbia Insurance
    Department
613 G Street, N.W.
Room 619
P.O. Box 37200
Washington, DC 20001-7200
(202) 727-8017

Florida
Florida Department of Insurance
State Capitol
Plaza Level Eleven
Tallahassee, FL 32399-0300
Toll-free (within state)
    1-800-342-2762
(904) 488-0030

Georgia
Georgia Insurance Department
2 Martin L. King, Jr., Drive
Room 716, West Tower
Atlanta, GA 30334
(404) 656-2056

Guam
Guam Insurance Department
855 W. Marine Drive
P.O. Box 2796
Agana, Guam 96910
011-671-477-1040

Hawaii
Hawaii Department of Commerce
    and Consumer Affairs
Insurance Division
P.O. Box 3614
Honolulu, HI 96811
(808) 548-5450

Idaho
Idaho Insurance Department
Public Service Department
500 South 10th Street
Boise, ID 83720
(208) 334-3102

Illinois
Illinois Insurance Department
320 West Washington Street
4th Floor
Springfield, IL 62767
(217) 782-4515

Indiana
Indiana Insurance Department
311 W. Washington Street
Suite 300
Indianapolis, IN 46204
(317) 232-2395

Iowa
Iowa Insurance Division
Lucas State Office Building
Suite 300, 6th Floor
East 12th and Grand Streets
Des Moines, IA 50319
(515) 281-5705

Kansas
Kansas Insurance Department
420 Southwest 9th Street
Topeka, KS 66612
(913) 296-3071

Kentucky
Kentucky Insurance Department
229 West Main Street
P.O. Box 517
Frankfort, KY 40602
(502) 564-3630

Louisiana
Louisiana Insurance Department
P.O. Box 94214
Baton Rouge, LA 70804-9214
(504) 342-5900

Maine
Maine Bureau of Insurance
Consumer Division
State House, Station 34
Augusta, ME 04333
(207) 582-8707

Maryland
Maryland Insurance Department
Complaints and Investigation Unit
501 St. Paul Place
Baltimore, MD 21202-2272
(301) 333-2792

Massachusetts
Massachusetts Insurance Division
Consumer Services Section
280 Friend Street
Boston, MA 02114
(617) 727-7189

Michigan
Michigan Insurance Department
P.O. Box 30220
Lansing, MI 48909
(517) 373-0220

Minnesota
Minnesota Insurance Department
Department of Commerce
133 E. 7th Street
St. Paul, MN 55101
(612) 296-4026

Mississippi
Mississippi Insurance Department
Consumer Assistance Division
P.O. Box 79
Jackson, MS 39205
(601) 359-3569

Missouri
Missouri Division of Insurance
Consumer Services Section
P.O. Box 690
Jefferson City, MO 65102-0690
(314) 751-2640

Montana
Montana Insurance Department
Mitchell Building
126 North Sanders, Room 270
P.O. Box 4009
Helena, MT 59604
Toll-free (within state)
1-800-332-6148
(406) 444-2040

Nebraska
Nebraska Insurance Department
Terminal Building
941 O Street, Suite 400
Lincoln, NE 68508
(402) 471-2201

Nevada
Nevada Department of Commerce
Insurance Division, Consumer
    Section
1665 Hot Springs Road
Capitol Complex
Carson City, NV 89701
(702) 687-4270

New Hampshire
New Hampshire Insurance
    Department
Life and Health Division
169 Manchester Street
Concord, NH 03301
(603) 271-2261

New Jersey
New Jersey Insurance Department
20 West State Street
Roebling Building
Trenton, NJ 08625
(609) 292-4757

New Mexico
New Mexico Insurance
    Department
P.O. Box 1269
Santa Fe, NM 87504-1269
(505) 827-4500

New York
New York Insurance Department
160 West Broadway
New York, NY 10013
New York City (212) 602-0203
Toll-free (within state, outside
    NYC) 1-800-342-3736

North Carolina
North Carolina Insurance
    Department
Consumer Services
Dobbs Building
P.O. Box 26387
Raleigh, NC 27611
(919) 733-2004

North Dakota
North Dakota Insurance
    Department
Capitol Building
5th Floor
Bismark, ND 58505
(701) 224-2440

Ohio
Ohio Insurance Department
Consumer Services Division
2100 Stella Court
Columbus, OH 43266-0566
(614) 644-2673

Oklahoma
Oklahoma Insurance Department
P.O. Box 53408
Oklahoma City, OK 73152-3408
(405) 521-2828

Oregon
Oregon Department of Insurance
and Finance
Insurance Division/Consumer
Advocate
21 Labor and Industry Building
Salem, OR 97310
(503) 378-4484

Pennsylvania
Pennsylvania Insurance
Department
1326 Strawberry Square
Harrisburg, PA 17120
(717) 787-2317

Puerto Rico
Puerto Rico Insurance
Department
Fernandez Juncos Station
P.O. Box 8330
Santurce, PR 00910
(809) 722-8686

Rhode Island
Rhode Island Insurance Division
233 Richmond Street, Suite 233
Providence, RI 02903-4233
(401) 277-2223

South Carolina
South Carolina Insurance
Department
P.O. Box 100105
Columbia, SC 29202-3105
(803) 737-6140

South Dakota
South Dakota Insurance
Department
Consumer Assistance Section
910 E. Sioux Avenue
Pierre, SD 57501-3940
(605) 773-3563

Tennessee
Tennessee Department of
Commerce and Insurance
Policyholders Service Section
500 James Robertson Parkway,
4th Floor
Nashville, TN 37243-0582
Toll-free (within state)
1-800-342-4029
(615) 741-4955

Texas
Texas Board of Insurance
Complaints Division
1110 San Jacinto Boulevard
Austin, TX 78701-1998
(512) 463-6501

Utah
Utah Insurance Department
Consumer Services
3110 State Office Building
Salt Lake City, UT 84114
(801) 530-6400

Vermont
Vermont Department of
Insurance and Banking
Consumer Complaint Division
120 State Street
Montpelier, VT 05602
(802) 828-3301

Virgin Islands
Virgin Islands Insurance
  Department
Kongens Garde No. 18
St. Thomas, VI 00802
(809) 774-2991

Virginia
Virginia Insurance Department
Consumer Services Division
700 Jefferson Building
P.O. Box 1157
Richmond, VA 23209
(804) 786-7691

Washington
Washington Insurance Department
Insurance Building AQ21
Olympia, WA 98504-0321
Toll-free (within state)
  1-800-562-6900
(206) 753-7300

West Virginia
West Virginia Insurance
  Department
2019 Washington Street, East
Charleston, WV 25305
(304) 348-3386

Wisconsin
Wisconsin Insurance Department
Complaints Department
P.O. Box 7873
Madison, WI 53707
(608) 266-0103

Wyoming
Wyoming Insurance Department
Herschler Building
122 W. 25th Street
Cheyenne, WY 82002
(307) 777-7401

APPENDIX B

This list contains the addresses of trial lawyer associations, found in all states. Many of these associations have referral services that will provide the names and telephone numbers of individual lawyers who are experienced in handling insurance claims on behalf of policyholders.

ALABAMA TRIAL LAWYERS ASSOCIATION
750 Washington Avenue
Suite 210
Montgomery, AL 36104
(205) 262-4974

ALASKA TRIAL LAWYERS ASSOCIATION
805 West 3rd Avenue
Suite A
Anchorage, AK 99501
(907) 258-4040

ARIZONA TRIAL LAWYERS ASSOCIATION
1001 North Central Avenue
Suite 590
Phoenix, AZ 85004
(602) 257-4040

ARKANSAS TRIAL LAWYERS ASSOCIATION
1700 First Commercial Building
Little Rock, AR 72201
(501) 372-5847

CALIFORNIA ASSOCIATION OF TRIAL LAWYERS
1020 Twelfth Street, 4th Floor
Sacramento, CA 95814
(916) 442-6902

LOS ANGELES TRIAL LAWYERS ASSOCIATION
2140 West Olympic Boulevard
Suite 324
Los Angeles, CA 90006
(213) 487-1212

ORANGE COUNTY TRIAL LAWYERS ASSOCIATION
888 North Main Street
Suite 905
Santa Ana, CA 92701
(714) 836-7791

SAN DIEGO TRIAL LAWYERS ASSOCIATION
2247 San Diego Avenue
Suite 136
San Diego, CA 92110
(619) 299-7757

SAN FRANCISCO TRIAL LAWYERS ASSOCIATION
World Trade Center
Ferry Building
Suite 230
San Francisco, CA 94111
(415) 956-6401

COLORADO TRIAL LAWYERS ASSOCIATION
1888 Sherman Street
Suite 370
Denver, CO 80203
(303) 831-1192

CONNECTICUT TRIAL LAWYERS ASSOCIATION
563 Broad Street
Hartford, CT 06106
(203) 522-4345

DELAWARE TRIAL LAWYERS ASSOCIATION
P.O. Box 1145
Wilmington, DE 19899
(302) 652-6635

TRIAL LAWYERS ASSOCIATION OF THE DISTRICT OF COLUMBIA
1818 N Street, NW
Suite 250
Washington, DC 20036
(202) 659-3532

THE ACADEMY OF FLORIDA TRIAL LAWYERS
218 South Monroe Street
Tallahassee, FL 32301
(904) 224-9403

GEORGIA TRIAL LAWYERS ASSOCIATION
41 Marietta Street
Suite 714
Atlanta, GA 30303
(404) 522-8487

IDAHO TRIAL LAWYERS ASSOCIATION
P.O. Box 1777
Boise, ID 83701
(208) 345-1890

ILLINOIS TRIAL LAWYERS ASSOCIATION
110 West Edwards Street
P.O. Box 5000
Springfield, IL 62705
(217) 789-0755

INDIANA TRIAL LAWYERS ASSOCIATION
309 West Washington Street
Suite 207
Indianapolis, IN 46204
(317) 634-8841

ASSOCIATION OF TRIAL LAWYERS OF IOWA
526 Fleming Building
Des Moines, IA 50309
(515) 280-7366

KANSAS TRIAL LAWYERS ASSOCIATION
112 West Sixth Street
Suite 311
Topeka, KS 66603
(913) 232-7756

**KENTUCKY ACADEMY OF
TRIAL LAWYERS**
200 Cumberland Building
12700 Shelbyville Road
Louisville, KY 40243
(502) 244-1320

**LOUISIANA TRIAL LAWYERS
ASSOCIATION**
442 Europe Street
P.O. Drawer 4289
Baton Rouge, LA 70821
(504) 383-5554

**MAINE TRIAL LAWYERS
ASSOCIATION**
34 Parkwood Drive
P.O. Box 428
Augusta, ME 04330
(207) 623-2661

**MARYLAND TRIAL LAWYERS
ASSOCIATION**
201 East Preston Street
Baltimore, MD 21202
(301) 539-4336

**MASSACHUSETTS ACADEMY
OF TRIAL LAWYERS**
59 Temple Place
Suite 410
Boston, MA 02111
(617) 350-0146

**MICHIGAN TRIAL LAWYERS
ASSOCIATION**
501 South Capitol Avenue
Suite 405
Lansing, MI 48933
(517) 482-7740

**MINNESOTA TRIAL LAWYERS
ASSOCIATION**
906 Midwest Plaza East
Minneapolis, MN 55402
(612) 375-1707

**MISSISSIPPI TRIAL LAWYERS
ASSOCIATION**
727 North Congress Street
P.O. Box 1992
Jackson, MS 39205
(601) 948-8631

**MISSOURI ASSOCIATION OF
TRIAL LAWYERS**
312 Monroe Street
2nd Floor
P.O. Box 1792
Jefferson City, MO 65102
(314) 635-5215

**MONTANA TRIAL LAWYERS
ASSOCIATION**
#1 Last Chance Gulch
Helena, MT 59601
(406) 443-3124

**NEBRASKA ASSOCIATION OF
TRIAL LAWYERS**
605 South 14th Street
Suite 450A
Lincoln, NE 68508
(402) 435-5526

**NEVADA TRIAL LAWYERS
ASSOCIATION**
205 South Minnesota Street
Carson City, NV 89703
(702) 883-3577

NEW HAMPSHIRE TRIAL LAWYERS ASSOCIATION
2½ Beacon Street
P.O. Box 447
Concord, NH 03302
(603) 224-7077

ASSOCIATION OF TRIAL LAWYERS OF AMERICA— NEW JERSEY
15 South Main Street
Edison, NJ 08837
(201) 906-8444

NEW MEXICO TRIAL LAWYERS ASSOCIATION
P.O. Box 301
Albuquerque, NM 87103
(505) 243-6003

NEW YORK STATE TRIAL LAWYERS ASSOCIATION, INC.
132 Nassau Street
New York, NY 10038
(212) 349-5890

NORTH CAROLINA ACADEMY OF TRIAL LAWYERS
208 Fayetteville Mall
P.O. Box 767
Raleigh, NC 27602
(919) 832-1413

NORTH DAKOTA TRIAL LAWYERS ASSOCIATION
P.O. Box 2359
Bismarck, ND 58502
(701) 258-9530

OHIO ACADEMY OF TRIAL LAWYERS
1024 Dublin Road
Columbus, OH 43215
(614) 488-3151

OKLAHOMA TRIAL LAWYERS ASSOCIATION
323 Northeast 27th
Oklahoma City, OK 73105
(405) 525-8044

OREGON TRIAL LAWYERS ASSOCIATION
1020 Southwest Taylor Street
Suite 750
Portland, OR 97205
(503) 223-5587

PENNSYLVANIA TRIAL LAWYERS ASSOCIATION
230 South Broad Street
18th Floor
Philadelphia, PA 19102
(215) 546-6451

PHILADELPHIA TRIAL LAWYERS ASSOCIATION
230 South Broad Street
18th Floor
Philadelphia, PA 19102
(215) 732-2256

RHODE ISLAND TRIAL LAWYERS ASSOCIATION
12 Barnes Street
Smithfield, RI 02828
(401) 272-8855

**SOUTH CAROLINA TRIAL
LAWYERS ASSOCIATION**
P.O. Box 11557
Columbia, SC 29211
(803) 799-5097

**SOUTH DAKOTA TRIAL
LAWYERS ASSOCIATION**
207 East Capitol
Suite 206
P.O. Box 1154
Pierre, SD 57501
(605) 224-9292

**TENNESSEE TRIAL LAWYERS
ASSOCIATION**
629 Woodland Street
Nashville, TN 37206
(615) 254-1986

**TEXAS TRIAL LAWYERS
ASSOCIATION**
1220 Colorado
Austin, TX 78701
(512) 476-3852

**UTAH TRIAL LAWYERS
ASSOCIATION**
141 West Haven Avenue
Suite 2
Salt Lake City, UT 84115
(801) 487-4841

**VERMONT TRIAL LAWYERS
ASSOCIATION**
P.O. Box 5359
Burlington, VT 05402
(802) 865-4700

**VIRGINIA TRIAL LAWYERS
ASSOCIATION**
700 East Main Street
Suite 1510
Richmond, VA 23219
(804) 343-1143

**WASHINGTON STATE TRIAL
LAWYERS ASSOCIATION**
225 South Washington
Seattle, WA 98104
(206) 464-1011

**WEST VIRGINIA TRIAL
LAWYERS ASSOCIATION**
P.O. Box 3968
Charleston, WV 25339
(304) 344-0692

**WISCONSIN ACADEMY OF
TRIAL LAWYERS**
44 East Mifflin Street
Madison, WI 53703
(608) 257-5741

**WYOMING TRIAL LAWYERS
ASSOCIATION**
2601 Central Avenue
Suite 100
Cheyenne, WY 82001
(307) 635-0820

**TRIAL LAWYERS
ASSOCIATION OF BRITISH
COLUMBIA**
464-1155 West Georgia Street
Vancouver, British Columbia
Canada V6E 3H4
(604) 682-5343

**SASKATCHEWAN TRIAL
LAWYERS ASSOCIATION**
137 Meighen Crescent
Saskatoon, Saskatchewan
Canada S7L 4W3
(306) 382-8663

Mr. Shernoff's law firm in Claremont, California, has a staff of insurance analysts who will assist policyholders and answer questions concerning insurance coverage and disputes. Correspondence can be directed to Insurance Analysts, Shernoff, Bidart & Darras, 600 South Indian Hill Boulevard, Claremont, CA 91711-5498; or policyholders can call (714) 621-4935.

Index